P9-CML-906

Alternative Worship

Alternative Worship

Resources from and for the Emerging Church

Compiled by **Jonny Baker** and **Doug Gay**
with **Jenny Brown**

 Baker Books

A Division of Baker Book House Co
Grand Rapids, Michigan 49516

© 2003 Jonny Baker and Doug Gay

Published 2004 by Baker Books
a division of Baker Book House Company
P.O. Box 6287, Grand Rapids, MI 49516-6287
www.bakerbooks.com

First published in Great Britain in 2003 by Society for Promoting Christian Knowledge, Holy Trinity Church, Marylebone Road, London NW1 4DU

Library of Congress Cataloging-in-Publication Data
Baker, Jonny.
  Alternative worship : resources from and for the emerging church / compiled by Jonny Baker and Doug Gay with Jenny Brown.
      p.   cm.
  Originally published : London : Society for Promoting Christian Knowledge, 2003.
  Includes bibliographical references (p.   ) and index.
  ISBN 0-8010-9170-5
  1. Worship programs. 2. Church year. I. Gay, Doug. II. Brown, Jenny. III. Title.
BV198.B25 2004
264—dc22   2003020920

To all the companions on the way, especially in Grace, the Late, Late Service and at HOST, and with sincere thanks to Youth for Christ and Thames North Synod of the URC whose Creativity Scholarship enabled time to be given to this project.

Contents

Foreword

It was early 1997. I had been facilitating corporate worship for twelve years—researching, writing, and speaking about it for ten. From the late-1980s to mid-1990s, the shifts in North American worship style and practice had been nothing short of tectonic. The praise and worship model propelled from the outer fringes (Vineyards, Calvary Chapels, independent charismatic fellowships) to become the primary worship expression in contemporary evangelical and mainline services. By 1995, the first UK revival CDs were just hitting the North American market, soon to jumpstart an astonishing youth worship phenomenon. The concept of worship as witness was rapidly gaining momentum while entertainment-based seeker services—once the darling of the church growth world—were adding praise choruses and prayers just to keep up.

Still, as many North American churches reveled in the so-called worship revolution, I sensed that what we were creating was, once again, a club activity for the inner circle, certainly not sacred space hospitable to aliens (definition: those oh-so spiritually active coresidents of our planet). With each passing year, it was becoming clear that what we deemed contemporary was but a subcultural tweak on essentially modern forms: services that, whether intentionally or unintentionally, abstracted God from street-level human experience. Where the rest of North American culture seemed increasingly bent on reenchanting the world through art, movement, symbol, pop culture, and just about anything ancient redux (think Cirque du Soleil, Blue Man Group, Winter Olympic prayer-on-ice ceremonies, and post-TWA crash memorial shrines), our blocky, denuded worship spaces seemed just as bent on doing the opposite. Where multitextured, iconic feasts were becoming the norm in film,

9

television news, concerts, sports events, and the Internet, contemporary worship remained—to great degree—a sensory wasteland, priding itself especially on visual asceticism: white-on-blue song lyrics interspersed with impossibly pristine nature imagery, and, of course, the ubiquitous church logo.

Surely, congregations in countries further down the postmodern pike must be ahead of us in the attempt to recapture an expanded sense of the sacred—a surety that God is not confined to closed-eyed praise choruses (out there, somewhere, ephemeral, unimaged); a confidence that God is actually embedded in what we see, hear, touch, taste, and smell every day. Surely there is a gathering of Christians somewhere who not only understand but practice incarnation, faithful to a God who voluntarily breaches heaven and earth precisely to *image* the image-less; to put the face of the Son on the eternal. Surely there are believers who take Philippians 2:4–11 seriously, this incomprehensible Creator who meets us full on, full-fleshed in our material, sensory, and consummately mundane space: mangers, drugs, sex addictions, racial conflict, computer viruses, techno music, traffic jams, and all.

Thus, one wintry March day, I began a computer search for what my intuition told me had to exist—worship expressions that not only baptize the emotions and the vocal chords but revive the spiritual imagination and reconnect the divine to the everyday. I was looking for the church unapologetically responsive to the postmodern context; the church freed to embrace all five senses, unafraid to unearth historic worship forms and catapult them into the twenty-first century. In short, the church whose mission it was to re-enchant God for an increasingly sophisticated but disenchanted world.

I entered word combinations such as, "new+sacramental," "worship+digital+art," "ancient+electronic," "liturgy+postmodern." What followed was a site-by-site, e-mail-by-e-mail journey with visionaries, leaders, and artists from the alternative (alt) worship movement, primarily centered in the UK, New Zealand, and Australia. Their web sites were intoxicating—digital tapestries of images, worship experiences, indigenous litanies, poetry, multi-sensory experiments, communal histories, and club (rave) postings. With names like Holyspace, Scriptorium, Embody, Labyrinth, Sanctus, Proost, Small Fire, Visions, The Mass, Vaux, and Paradox, they oozed a mystical, pre-modern ancestry known only to Americans via *Becket* and *Braveheart*. When contrasted with the intentionally a-historic, sandwich-board nomenclature of contemporary churchland in the States (Celebration Community, New Life Christian, Beachside Family Center), I was struck with just how far down the postmodern pike these alt communities really were.

About six months into my cyber, alt-worship journey, I ran across a reference to a video entitled, *God in the House,* a BBC production featuring several alt worship gatherings around the UK. A few rabbit trails later, I finally connected with someone named Andy who said he had an extra copy he'd stick in the mail. The day the video came, I canceled my afternoon meeting just so I could watch it. With all my meanderings into the alt worship world, I was still unprepared for what I saw.

Most riveting was a twenty-minute clip of the "Late Late Service," a Christmas Eve mass brilliantly contextualized for a rave community in Glasgow, Scotland. The space was old, gothic, but smallish. Accustomed as I was to flat-ceilinged, strip-mall church plants, the place seemed positively cathedralesque. A mélange of film loops on stacked television monitors, candles, ambient techno, stained glass, triangular fabric screens, throbbing house beat, vernacular litanies, icons, and intimate rituals, here was the ancient spilling freely, instinctively into the unequivocal now.

The gathering was surprisingly miniscule, no more than fifty people. But what it lacked in sheer units it made up for in diversity. From black-leathered clubbers, middle-aged hippies, mothers dancing with babies, to thirty-something collared-types—this was about as far from church-growth homogeneous one could get. The arrangement of the space was bizarre by contemporary standards. No platform, no singing Master of Ceremony with head-set, guitar, and bleached-perfect smile. Indeed, there was no "front" at all, no sanctified dais where supposed worship experts performed and pontificated. Instead, a community of leaders—both men and women—traded off, facilitating a locus of activity that shifted from center to side, dispersed in small groupings, then back to center. The pews had been removed, participants encountering God and each other in a host of ways:

- dancing to a thumping "O Come, O Come Emmanuel"
- passing an enormous candle—torch-like—as they danced
- holding hands in a large circle while intoning the words of the Anglican mass
- engaging in a unity ritual with candles and a crock of sand
- arranging the elements of the Lord's Supper—complete with icons, old and new—on an old table (hefted in even as the singing continued)
- administering the Eucharist to each other in pairs

Most intriguing to me, however, was the corporate confession at the very beginning: a postmodern, techno-undergirded Kyrie, boldly enumerating before God and each other areas of neglect, selfishness, acquiescence, and apathy within their community.

AUTHOR OF CREATION LITANY

Leader: We confess that we live in an age that what a person has can
be seen as more important than who they are.

In an attempt to have, we are in danger of losing our very
selves.

In an attempt to have, we have left many on the margins of
society.

All: (sung) Author of creation, we cannot see your face

Have mercy on our blindness, send to us a sign of grace.

Leader: We confess that we run around seeking comfort and security,
but we have failed to go on our own spiritual journeys.

In doing this, we have sacrificed relationships and justice for
personal passions. We've been wrong, we've been deluded,
we're sorry.

All: (sung): Author of creation, we cannot see your face

Have mercy on our blindness, send to us a sign of grace.

Leader: We confess that we live in an age where trust is in short supply;

Where the press tells us all that there is to fear and we hide in
our fortress homes.

We have failed to foster compassion and left the vulnerable
uncared for.

We've been wrong, we've been deluded, we're sorry.

Say and receive these words of forgiveness:

All: God, who is both power and love,

Forgive us and free us from our sins

Heal and strengthen us by the Spirit

And raise us to new life in Christ our Lord.

I watched the Late, Late Service four times—mesmerized. The next
week I began showing it in seminars across the country. The reactions of
seminar attendees were nearly as fascinating as the material. In evangelical
circles, a few attendees labeled the service cultish, citing the dancing and
visual elements. More than a few of their peers, however, alluded to the
rich theological content, some claiming the service was more "trinitarian

and God-centered" than their own praise services. In mainline circles, the reaction was quietly ecstatic. Without prompting, Methodists, Lutherans, Presbyterians, Episcopalians, Disciples of Christ, etc., recognized the worship form and substance for what it was: the ancient Christian mass—the *Missio De*—radically reconfigured.

I traveled with this *God in the House* tape and played it across the country at pastoral and worship conferences until it literally shredded in a dusty church basement machine. Alas, the tape was gone, but the service as well as the "a-ha!" moments at conferences remain fresh in my memory. Here were leaders from every Christian denomination conceivable, transfixed by a world they'd never hoped to imagine, much less see. The anticipation for what creativity and theological depth like this might mean in their worship ministries was almost palpable. Their body language changed as they watched. Some leaned forward in their chairs, elbows on knees, chins on hands, intent. Others straightened in their chairs, eyes wide, heads nodding slowly in silent affirmation. Still others drew closer to their staff mates and whispered like school kids. It was as if there was a collective sigh of relief. As one attendee remarked, "Finally, something that takes us beyond five choruses of 'Shout to the Lord' and a talking head!"

I still receive e-mails from leaders asking where they can get a copy of the Glasgow video. How ironic that this alternative gathering was filmed in 1993! (Our ministry friends across both oceans must be having a good chuckle over the cultural lag!) Yet, even if it had been filmed in 2003, the point is well taken: North America is not Glasgow. Neither is it Auckland or Sydney. Truly, the Incarnate God comes to us in the particular, not the formulaic. And we of all people on the planet should know this, having experienced over two decades of church franchising and seeing ever-decreasing results. Like megacorporations, we simply learned how to empty out the mom and pop shops and fill big box stores.

No, North America is not Europe, Australia, or New Zealand. That being said, we are following fast in their post-Christendom footsteps. Data coming from several studies redraws an America where the church is moving quickly into exile. As early as 1996, the North American Society for Church Growth reported that no county in the United States had a greater percentage of churched people than it had had ten years earlier.[1] Ironically, these years were the so-called golden years of the church movement. A behavioral study conducted in 1998 estimated U.S. church attendance at 26 percent rather than the 40 percent claimed by pollsters since the sixties. One can't help but wonder what the attendance figure would be if this study were revisited post-millennium. Conducted by sociologist Stanley Presser of the University of Maryland and research assistant Linda Stinson of the U.S. Bureau of

Labor Statistics, this indepth analysis of diary entries from 1960–1990 netted
a discrepancy between religious behavior journaled and what the average
American told pollsters about his or her church attendance—a discrepancy
that inflated church-going figures by about 30 percent. Presser and Stinson
also found that the percentage of Americans who lie about their attendance
is increasing. As to the reason people lie about how often they go to church,
Presser and Stinson speculated, "Respondents felt the need to inflate their
church attendance to impress the interviewers."[2]

Researchers C. Kirk Hadaway and Penny Marler would agree with
Presser and Stinson's assessment. "If the poll data can be believed, three
decades of otherwise corrosive social and cultural change has left American
church attendance virtually untouched. . . . Numerous studies show that
people do not accurately report their behavior to pollsters. Americans
misreport how often they vote, how much they give to charity, and how
frequently they use illegal drugs. Their misreporting is in the expected
direction: People report higher than actual figures for voting and charitable
giving, lower for illegal drug use. We should not expect religious behavior
to be immune to such misreporting." Hadaway and Marler's study, based
on attendance counts in Protestant churches in one Ohio county and
Catholic churches in eighteen dioceses, also indicated a much lower rate
of religious participation than the telephone polls report. Instead of 40
percent of Protestants attending church, they found 20 percent. Instead
of 50 percent of Catholics attending church, they found 28 percent. In
other words, actual church attendance was about half the rate indicated
by yearly phone surveys.[3]

Church attendance isn't the only religious indicator that is plummeting in
the new world. So are the public opinion polls. Recently, the Gallup Index
of Leading Religious Indicators showed that the overall public opinion rating
for organized religion plunged to its lowest level in more than six decades.[4]
In another recent opinion poll—this time, querying non-Christians—The
Barna Research Group reported that only 44 percent of this group have positive views of clergy; only one-third (32 percent) have a positive impression
of born-again Christians, and just one-fifth (22 percent) have a positive view
of evangelicals.[5]

If we are to take these studies seriously, our 1980s "if we build it, they will
come" formulas are nothing short of ludicrous. In a post-Christendom context—the North American Church lacking even the most basic connectedness
into its communities—the more relevant question is, If we build it, who cares?
Given the articles about antichurch zoning laws that are sprouting up in local
papers all over the United States, the only unchurched people who care if a

congregation is erecting a megacampus are the neighbors who have to put up with the parking and the congestion. And they're saying, No thanks.

In light of our new, post-Christian reality, it is absolutely crucial that North American ministry leaders shift their focus from church growth, i.e., "being the best show in town" to kingdom growth via transforming their local communities. Bottom line, every local congregation has an appointment with the postmodern transition going on in its own backyard. Besides the gospel of Jesus Christ, the primary assets we as the church are given are two coordinates: a specific point on the time line and a specific point on the planet. It is up to us whether we will take these divinely established coordinates seriously. Indianapolis is not Edinburgh and no amount of candles, stacked television monitors, or candle-in-sand rituals will ever make it so.

Fortunately, there are signs that the franchised ministry frenzy of late twentieth century ministry is abating. A "neo-incarnation" of the gospel is beginning on new world soil—fledgling, perhaps, but beginning nonetheless. With a heightened attention to things local, I would like to think that the current North American interest in the alternative worship movement has more to do with things intrinsic than extrinsic—a weightiness of worship substance, a well-rooted ecclesiology, and a persistent cultural "archeology." As I read this elegantly accessible resource, Alternative Worship, and culled from miscellaneous blogs and alternative worship web sites, I came up with this summary of what seem to be the movement's most intrinsic worship values:

- Faithful improvisation (the intentioned, informed reframing of tradition)
- Worship focused on the triune person of God and the acts of God through history, not primarily on how worshipers feel or think or what they need
- Profound versus superficial engagement with postmodern/popular culture (an engagement, which at base, involves the clear affirmation of God's sovereign presence in all of life)
- Worship that emerges out of a lived community versus worship that merely parrots a model
- Worship that reflects a transforming, resistant presence of the church in the world
- Commitment to:
    reveal, respond to, and experience God through all the arts, not just music
    excavate the rich deposits of visual history, including icons past and present

creativity
craft worship collaboratively
provide tools for honest encounters with God (lament, confession, meditation, silence, undoctored story)
open-ended versus outcome-based responses
diversity over homogeneous

The question becomes, what of the alternative worshiping communities can we as North Americans borrow and still be, well, North American, whether that be Lancaster, Ashville, Des Moines, Madison, Colorado Springs, Austin, Portland, or Torrance? Perhaps it is the inherent principles listed above that we really need to internalize and then shape through our own cultural languages: jazz, salsa, R and B, hip hop, merengue, gospel, urban Chicago graffiti, or Seattle digital pastiche. If alternative worship is only germane to twenty-somethings, club communities in places like Glasgow or Leeds, then most of us could put this book back on the shelf without a nano-second's thought.

If, however, the alternative worship movement is much less about the trendy trappings of postmodern Europe and the down-under than a laser-like apprehension of Christian theology, ecclesiology, and missiology, we'd better sit up and take notice. And, in my estimation, the latter is most definitely the case. For in drafty cathedrals, makeshift warehouse space, boxy back-alley coffee-houses, and smoke-filled pubs, alt worshipers have been hammering out what it is to be the gathered people of God—postscientism, postrational-ism, and, most importantly, post-Christendom; what it is to be the church in exile: dispersed, disenfranchised, unsanctioned, unwelcome; what it is to worship God when gods are ubiquitous and every god-story, valid. And what it is to bridge boldly back into this new world—post-Christian, deconstructed, fragmented—with the Savior's embodied love.

For North American believers to bridge into this new world—post-Christian, deconstructed, fragmented, and profoundly disinterested in things religious—it will take congregations that live their worship as a transforming presence in their communities and whose sacred gatherings are in natural resonance with the lives they live as the people of God, seven days a week. The days of dressing up and using worship services as image management are over.

Alongside this radicalized authenticity, however, must come an unmitigated commitment to the historic task of worship: *seeing God for who God is and ourselves for who we truly are.* This is the holy realignment that must happen, not only if worship is to be worship, but also if the church is to have any sure antidote to self-absorption, self-congratulation, and self-destruction. As *Alterna-*

tive Worship's postmodern liturgies express so lucidly, worship celebrates the Unparalleled Who of the Grand Story. And as we celebrate the Subject of our faith—Creator, Redeemer, and Sanctifier—we enter into the rhythms and seasons of God's activity in our world, past, present, and future. Finally, held centripetally by the unchanging nature of this One we worship, we can affirm to God and to each other who we really are: a wildly gifted and profoundly flawed people in the marvelous, mystical process of redemption.

If there is immediate application to North American churches from our alternative brothers and sisters across both ponds, it is this: The indigenous, accessible call to realignment with the One Who Was, Is, and Is Still to Come: a call made audible and compelling, not only through the fresh-hewn pathways of the now, but the well-traveled conduits of the past. Thank you, Jonny Baker, Jenny Brown, and Doug Gay, for sounding this divine call and sounding it faithfully. May we too respond in faithfulness.

Sally Morgenthaler, founder, Sacramentis.com

Introduction

This is a collection of resources from and for "the emerging church." It is not a large-scale blueprint for change—it is a collection of resources and reports from more than a decade of experimenting with alt worship in the UK. The Peruvian liberation theologian Gustavo Gutiérrez talks of theology as a second moment—one which comes after "praxis"—a moment in which the people of God reflect on what they have been doing in a way which will help to shape what they are about to do. The reflections we have included are born out of our experience and the resources are drawn from our practice—both are offered to the wider church for evaluation and use.

WHO'S ALTERNATIVE?

The bit of the church's practice we are dealing with here has already been given a name. The name "alt worship" is one many involved in it dislike, but it has stuck and it is still the most common term used to describe the range of experiments with new forms of worship inspired by the work of the Nine O'Clock Service. This pioneering project emerged in the late 1980s from an Anglican congregation in Sheffield, a major urban center in the North of England, with a vibrant urban music scene and dance club culture.

Looking back over a decade or so of alt worship there seem to be a number of reasons for the interest these experiments provoked.

- First, this was a surprising innovation in worship practice—few people saw it coming and the work of the pioneering group, Sheffield's Nine O'Clock Service (NOS), burst onto the UK church scene with little warning.

- Second, it appeared to be a successful innovation in church practice, offering new hopes for mission and church growth among a key group of alienated young adults at a time of crisis and decline in mainstream denominations.

- Third, as a way of enculturating worship (choosing particular cultural and aesthetic forms) it came close to riding the crest of a wave in popular culture; the musical and visual forms taken up were much more closely aligned with those in current use and vogue in the rest of society than has usually been the case in recent church history.[1]

A misconception in some circles has been that alt worship is primarily a youth ministry program—this is clearly not the case for most groups and many have been adamant that what they are doing is "church" and not youth ministry. It is easy to see why this has arisen. Often those working among young people, especially those outside of church, feel the irrelevance of the church most acutely. An incarnational and contextual approach to mission has gradually gained currency in youth ministry with studies in cross-cultural mission providing a fund for people's imagination and practice in outreach. The contextual approaches to worship being pioneered in alt worship are a natural progression and have offered some real clues for a way forward. Youth ministry has often been the back door to renewing the church (what takes place in youth ministry appears in the mainstream fifteen years later), so this cross-fertilization is very welcome (and there are many people involved in both, including one of the authors).

Before the name "alt worship" appeared, early experiments were being dubbed "rave worship" because they were borrowing directly from the culture of dance music in the late 1980s and early 1990s. In opting to introduce dance music into worship there was a clear continuity with a tradition of modernizing church music in line with popular culture which goes back through the era of the music hall to the work of Martin Luther and others in the Protestant Reformation. However, this particular exercise in modernizing church music came packaged with other more unexpected features.

IT'S SAFE TO DANCE

First of all, it brought "dance" into worship in a new way. Of course, the charismatic renewal had reintroduced dance to worship in UK churches from the late 1960s, both as performance (sacred dance) and as participation (dancing in the Spirit); there was also a significant presence of black-majority churches for many of whom some form of dancing in worship was unremarkable. Alt worship saw a different use of dance. It was "normal dance," "real dance" as opposed to churchy dance. This was perhaps more like a non-western use of dance in worship—people were dancing in church in the same way as they would dance in a club or at a rave. This forceful introduction of dance to worship, in its "unbaptized" and "profane" form, brought with it a whole set of questions about physicality and the body, which had been more implicitly and dualistically raised by the charismatic renewal. These were questions in search of theological answers.

PICTURE THIS

Alt worship also arrived with pictures. This again owed much to dance culture, in which raves were being held in increasingly complex and sophisticated visual environments. Despite widespread discussion of the significance of living in the age of television, which had been going on within the church since at least the 1950s, until the Nine O'Clock Service in the late '80s, very few people had made any significant links to a new electronic visual culture in their worship practice. When alt worship arrived bearing computer graphics, video, and slide projection, the churches had literally never seen anything like it. Overnight, worship practice had been launched into late twentieth-century visual culture. Again, given the history of debate within Christian tradition about the use of images in church (aniconic traditions and iconoclastic controversies) this also raised deep theological questions.

EVANGELICAL CATHOLICISM

Most alt worship groups emerged out of the mainstream of charismatic-evangelical Christianity in the UK, but they were also marked by the influence of other worship traditions, which might loosely be described as "catholic":

- One of the most significant of these influences was probably the Taizé Community, an ecumenical community based in France, which from the 1960s had a huge influence on worship culture worldwide, particularly among young people. Taizé offered a classic liturgical shape, a recycling of the ancient songs of the church, a revival in simple un-accompanied chanting, and a slightly eclectic use of ritual. Many alt services still make regular use of Taizé music in their worship.

- Another influence on some groups was the work of the Iona Commu-nity, an ecumenical community based in Scotland, whose Wild Goose Resource Group have published many new resources for worship over the past twenty years. They drew on Taizé music, but also supplemented it with a huge range of new worship songs, many of them settings of classic liturgical texts. They also pioneered creative and eclectic uses of ritual and liturgical action.

- For those groups working within the Anglican communion, there was a high church tradition near at hand which had preserved (or revived) the use of color, gesture, and ritual in worship practice.

The UK's leading Christian Arts Festival, Greenbelt, now thirty years old, gave space to groups to share their worship with a wider public. Out of the festi-val a fanzine, an internet site, an online discussion group, and several gatherings were spawned. Greenbelt's radical theological agenda and its commitment to social justice and the arts made it a natural home base for alt worship.

POST-MODERN WORSHIP?

The "alt" in alternative worship can be linked to the "post" in post-modern. It was alt/post to modernizing worship cultures.

Post-Charismatic

Alt worship was "post-charismatic," particularly in the determination of most groups to reject the culture of chorus singing and the worship group with worship leader. We have already noted the time lag between the musi-cal forms (soft rock; easy listening) adopted by the charismatic renewal and the forms current in "secular youth music." There was a reaction against a performance-based musical idiom, in favor of one oriented to communal celebration and participation. People were also reacting against a model of the working of the Holy Spirit which stressed immediacy, spontaneity, and extemporizing as the true signs of "the Spirit moving." The charismatic renewal contained an explicit critique of liturgical tradition as "formal therefore unfree." Most alt worship groups have rejected this opposition and turned back to embrace form, set prayers, and liturgical patterns. Both the turn from choruses and the turn from an exclusive emphasis on "free prayer" reflected an aesthetic and a spiritual disillusionment with these forms, a sense that they had produced a culture of banality in worship. A number of groups have retained a strong affinity with the theology of charismatic renewal, which they seek to explore within a new cultural mix.

Post-Evangelical

Another dimension of the alt reaction has something in common with the term "post-evangelical," which was much discussed on the UK church scene after the publication of Dave Tomlinson's book of that name in 1995.[2] If many in the groups came to faith in mainstream evangelical churches, they also show signs of having been influenced by a "radical evangelical" agenda—they are thoroughly politicized in relation to social justice and environmental issues and show strong commitment to gender equality. The relative lack of debate in alt worship groups over these issues contrasts with mainstream evangelical culture. There has also been a reaction against the tone of evangelical personal morality. The perception is that the evangelical emphasis on dogma and the right way to behave has often been at the expense of grace. Against a background of rising rates of divorce, a huge increase in couples living together, and an increasingly out gay and lesbian presence in society, evangelicals often come across to those outside as superior and judgmental. There is no one "alt" position on these issues (that would be missing the point though it would be fair to say some groups are more conservative, others more liberal), but the emphasis has shifted to creating communities of openness and grace where all are welcomed. Jesus' ministry of hospitality to sinners and outsiders has been a real source of inspiration.

Another "post-evangelical" feature is the insistence on the right to question and debate, sometimes in faintly adolescent terms. People were tired of the narrow parameters for theological discussion which they perceived to have been set in much of the evangelical world. Often the theology they had been schooled in seemed to be answering questions no one was asking, while contemporary concerns were simply not being addressed. One result was that new alliances and interactions were explored with non-evangelical traditions. Groups have sought to grow up theologically, rejecting the restrictive practices of over-protective church leaders who tried to protect their churches from unsound influences.

RE-SOURCING WORSHIP

We believe this theological journey has also been inspired by a genuinely missionary encounter with contemporary culture which has happened as groups experimented with new forms. The people planning and leading alt worship have been trying to make sense of what they were doing as they did it. This led them to new sources for guidance and inspiration:

History of Liturgy

The experience of many alt worshipers was like that of people suddenly discovering a birthright, a heritage which had been hidden from them. The riches of Catholic liturgical tradition were suddenly spread out before them, overflowing out of the old treasure chest: texts, chants, rituals, use of color, and gesture. The impact of these discoveries was to generate new respect for Catholic tradition, but this did not lead to any kind of anglo-catholic revivalism. Post-modern cultural savvy, combined with an evangelical tendency not to defer to high church regulation, led alt worshipers to treat this treasure chest as a kind of dressing-up box. Their appropriation of tradition was to be playful as well as serious and eclectic as well as respectful.

Media Studies/Fine Art/History of Art/Contemporary Art

Other people had been changing the beats and rhythms of worship for years. The truly distinctive thing about alt worship was that it arrived with a new appetite for imagery in worship and with new media for displaying it. This has been where some of the boldest and most exciting work has been done in the past ten years, but it has also been the area where there were fewest guides and teachers. Few clergy were skilled or trained in the visual arts, and few artists had developed theological and liturgical instincts. Some areas of the tradition were very well mapped—for example, the Orthodox use of icons and historical studies of religious art. Others were practically virgin territory. The use of photography and video as liturgical art forms was and still is in its infancy. The old ways of policing and editing worship were also thrown into confusion: What does visual orthodoxy mean? Or visual heresy?

Alt worship groups have also been concerned with prophetic "reading" of the visual culture around them in Western mass media. The work of subvertising agencies like Adbusters was being popularized and circulated between groups.[3] A generation attuned to media studies found they wanted to engage theologically with the critique of advertising as a form of social control and with emerging political critiques of representation and stereotyping. Their activism in setting up new worship services meant that this engagement was not just academic or literary but was enacted in the form and content of these services.

New Testament theologian Richard Bauckham writes in his study of the book of Revelation that the purpose of that work was "to purge and refurbish the Christian imagination" and that this work modeled a contemporary task for the church, which needed to be as contextual in our time as it was in the first century.[4] His statement offers a kind of dynamic manifesto for engagement with the arts in worship, which perhaps explains something of the intellectual, artistic, and prophetic challenge alt worship offered to what leading alt worship thinker Paul Roberts calls "those who would have stood out as obvious Christian leaders in more usual church contexts."[5]

New Religious Practice

Another Christian commentator whose work was influential for new worship groups was John Drane, now Professor of Practical Theology at the University of Aberdeen in Scotland, who was emerging as a leading UK figure critiquing the New Age movement and the churches' engagement with it. People in alt worship groups were reading Drane.[6] They were also influenced by the work of Richard Foster, in *Celebration of Discipline*; by Anthony de Mello's *Sadhana*; and more controversially by Matthew Fox's *Creation Spirituality*.

As many of our peers turned to various New Age options, went on courses in Buddhist meditation, and explored spirituality through electronic ambient environments in clubs, those of us involved in alt worship looked back into the contemplative spiritual traditions of Eastern and Western Christianity. The practice of many groups began to include guided meditation, visualization, and forms of physical prayer often using ambient music as a crucial dimension of the worship environment and experience.

The broader cultural search for new forms of spiritual experience formed a context within which groups were asking questions about the forms which had been offered to them within evangelical and charismatic Christianity. Again, few evangelicals were creatively and positively involved in mapping this territory. Alt worshipers sought out what sources they could, sharing and debating their worth on various internet forums, but often they had to be their own guides as they experimented with new forms of prayer and attentiveness to God.

Biblical Studies

While the role of the traditional sermon shifted dramatically in alt worship practice, most groups were still committed to serious engagement with the biblical text. Here again, new voices were influential: the work of Old Testament scholar Walter Brueggemann, *The Prophetic Imagination*, struck a chord with many groups, as did that of New Testament scholar Walter Wink, *Transforming Bible Study*. Writers like these were serious yet accessible; they were amenable to people raised in evangelical Bible studies but also showed a fresh sense of critical engagement with social, political, and cultural realities. Their methods also showed that they were in close dialogue with post-modern themes and voices. The increasing importance of literary criticism in biblical studies promoted the idea of "doing a reading" of the text which involved a heightened awareness of the reader's own cultural horizons. In 1994, the first volume of *Imaging the Word* appeared in the United States. This remarkable project was sponsored by the United Church of Christ and grew out of work at Yale and Texas Christian University. It offered a visual commentary on the lectionary, and as soon as it appeared it was seized upon by alt worshipers as a classic new resource for the territory in which they were working. It offered a stunning combination of historical depth and contemporary breadth. It was also a powerful exemplar of the alt worship desire for "reading the text through images."[7] Another important strand of biblical studies was the work of feminist scholars such as Elisabeth Schüssler Fiorenza and Phyllis Trible who stressed the distorting role of gender bias in reading biblical texts and revalued the experiences of women as a resource for rereading the Bible.

Liberation and Political Theology

Liberation theology had already touched churches in many places by the late 1980s, and most alt worship groups were marked by a more or less radicalized political agenda. A surprising number of alt worship founders had been influenced by the work of radical youth agency Frontier Youth Trust and FYT's theologian field worker Jim Punton's advocacy of liberation concerns in a UK context. Veteran Anglican activist Kenneth Leech was also a significant voice in this area and the work of Jürgen Moltmann in The Spirit of Life was taken up by NOS, LLS, and others. The songs and liturgies of Iona's Wild Goose Worship group were shot through with the influences of liberation theology and a new post-colonial awareness of belonging to the world church. The work of liturgist Janet Morley for relief agency Christian Aid was also an important model for many groups, and her prayers were widely used in services.

Feminist Theology

Alt worship groups have also been clearly influenced by feminist theology. While the technological elements were sometimes marked by a "toys for boys" mentality, women were a strong presence in alt worship congregations and leadership from the beginning. Some of the attraction for women seems to have been the willingness to renegotiate the politics of worship-leading in services. Many services worked hard at using inclusive language in their worship and female images and metaphors for God were used in songs and prayers.

POST-MODERN CHURCH

One of the distinctive features of alt worship has been a revival of interest in the worship traditions of the church. This contrasts with trends in the charismatic renewal, which was a "modernizing" move within church life and tended to take a more negative view of tradition. The interest in tradition was one of the factors in alt worship being labeled "post-modern," because of the way it combines the use of advanced mixed-media technology and techniques with an eclectic use of the worship traditions of the church. One way of understanding this is through the metaphor of "sampling" from music technology. In sampling, a slice of music is extracted from its original setting (whether a break beat from a James Brown song or a moment of the Hallelujah Chorus) and inserted into a new musical context, where it combines with other elements to form a new whole. The fact that alt worshipers sample liturgical tradition is not in itself new, since all new prayer books do something similar. What is distinctive about their approach is the way in which fragments of liturgical tradition—rituals, icons, chants, prayers, responses—are inserted into a mixed-media context. The juxtapositions have felt more radical because they have not simply been textual revisions of the old format, but have set up new links between liturgy and contemporary media.

Alt worship has also been shaped by broader currents of post-modern living. The practice of sampling feeds into the post-modern emphasis on continuous and shifting processes of constructing meanings. "Texts," whether they are written, visual, or aural, are wide open to interpretation, with interpreters unmasked as those who make meanings rather than merely uncovering or discovering them. This process of interpretation can be violent, suspicious, playful, and subversive—one "text" can be "read" through another "unlike" text. Post-modern theories of interpretation offer one way to describe what is happening when an alt worship service explores a theme simultaneously through the use of computer graphics and photographs of medieval religious paintings; through dance music with sampled quotes and fragments of the 1662 Anglican Communion Service; through continuous loops of silent TV ads backgrounding the gospel reading from a modern inclusive-language Bible, with another slide showing a page of the King James text for the same passage. Instead of full frontal pulpit/altar dominance, large screens construct a space within a space, a worship space with false walls and hidden depths; temporary icons are flashed up while the "real" monumental stained-glass sits obscurely in darkness 20 feet behind. The organist is a DJ. The vicar has been deconstructed. There is no front—people worship in the round—and the space is visually overdetermined (you cannot look at or take in everything at once), so you have to make your own meanings—even which direction you face in is a decision about making meaning.

WE ARE . . .

However shocking this can seem in church, alt worshipers can argue that we are all already more prepared for this than we know. Most of us are already coexisting blandly and blindly with a culture in which within 15 seconds we can move from watching a documentary on victims of landmines in Cambodia to watching a commercial for soft drinks; from a mindless game show, to tragic headlines in the nightly news. We do not blink an eyelid at preacher's rhetoric which can crack a joke at/with us and then cut us in mid-laugh with a story of sexual abuse, suicide, or cancer. Is this so different from watching a screen change from an image of the Simpsons to one of Saddam Hussein?

JUXTA-POSERS

Making alt worship (and attending it) has been an unwitting crash course in post-modern hermeneutics for many people—they have been asking and answering deep theological questions with their eyes and their bodies. Many of the juxtapositions occurring in services have been carefully planned, others have simply been stumbled on—some have happened for some worshipers and not for others. All have had to interact with the kaleidoscope of experience and attitude inside people's souls.

THIS BOOK/DISC

It should be obvious why a conventional book format would struggle to express the dimensions of alt worship practice, which is why we originally chose to work with the UK publisher SPCK, inspired by the success of their pioneering Prodigal Project book and CD. The CD-ROM is an essential part of the package—at a glance or a click, some of what has been described here will emerge from your screen and speakers and come to life. All the pieces in the book and CD-ROM—written pieces, rituals, images, music tracks, video loops, and animations—have been collated from various alt worship groups in the UK. We are incredibly grateful to them for their generosity and willingness to make these available to a wider audience. Thanks in particular to HOST (Hackney), Grace, Vaux, Visions, HOST (Bradford), Sanctuary (Bath), Resonance, Late Late Service, L8r, Home, and OSBD for taking the risk of trusting us. The pieces are loosely arranged to tie in with the seasons of the church calendar. Many of them were originally used in a service where a lot of other samples interacted with them. So as you read them use your imagination to see how they might be lifted off the page. Creativity and imagination are great gifts. Feel free to take and use these pieces in your worship. But make them your own, give them your own twist. There are also a series of short theological reflections throughout the book. These touch on some of the significant elements in alt worship (the use of liturgy, music, and images; the turn towards ritual; language; engagement with tradition and popular culture; the incarnation) and perhaps encapsulate what alt worship is attempting to do—faithful improvisation. We debated whether these reflections should be part of this book or published as something separate. But it felt as though the pieces and reflections belonged together. We hope that this book and CD-ROM provide a spark to your own creativity, enabling you to find your voice in worship and produce your own resources in fresh and imaginative ways if you are not doing so already.

Part 1

Advent and Christmas

Resources

The Christian year begins with Advent. The season of Advent (from a Latin root meaning "coming" or "arrival") runs through the four Sundays before Christmas. Advent is a time of preparation for the coming of Christ into the world, which traditionally both looks back to the first coming of Christ and also looks forward to the second coming or return of Christ.

These four weeks, like the six of Lent which formed a model for Advent as a liturgical device, are traditionally associated with spiritual disciplines of repentance, fasting, and waiting and are characterized by attitudes of longing and hope.

The movement of Advent is also a rich journey through the Bible. Each of the weeks has come to have strong associations with particular readings in which Christians trace the promise of the Messiah through the Hebrew Scriptures and are introduced to significant characters in the impending drama of the Christmas story. During Advent we wait with and through these characters and we hear their stories as witness: Elizabeth and Zechariah, John the Baptist, Mary and Joseph.

The Taizé book of common prayer says about Advent:

> Advent is a time of waiting in contemplation for the presence of Christ within us; we are called to bear Christ, to live Christ for others. We along with the witnesses are invited to live that same spirit of poverty, of humility and joy.

This suggests a mystical understanding of waiting above all with Mary; just as Christ is forming in her body, so we reflect on Christ being formed in our lives, coming again to us, to be born again in us.

CHRISTMAS

Christmas is presented by Catholic tradition as a period of festival and not just a single day—on Christmas Eve everything changes: the colors change from the purple of Advent to the white of Christmas; the mood changes from longing and expectation to joy and recognition; the song of the church changes from *Veni Immanuel* to *Hodie Christus Natus Est* (Christ is born today) with *alleluias* and *glorias* ringing out through the church's worship and liturgy.

The twelve days of Christmas, between Christmas Day and Epiphany, are days in which the significance of the birth increases rather than fades; they are always moving towards the Epiphany which celebrates the universal significance of Jesus' birth.

EPIPHANY

The season of Epiphany begins with the Feast of Epiphany traditionally celebrated on January 6.

* This feast is based on the visit of the Magi from the East recorded in Matthew's Gospel. The word Epiphany means "revealing" or "manifestation" and relates to this incident as a symbolic revealing of Jesus Christ to the Gentiles.
* Epiphany themes are expressed through the symbolism of "light" and relate to the universal mission of Christ and the church. Epiphany is an extrovert festival, a boundary-crossing, mind-broadening, commissioning moment for the church.

All of this, the longing of Advent, the arrival of Christmas, and the widening angle of Epiphany, prepare us spiritually and theologically to turn with fresh ears and eyes to the Gospels to look at Jesus' life and teaching once again.

Call to Worship

Relax your body . . .
Open your mind . . .
Engage your spirit . . .
This is the house of God
Prepare to worship.

Life is an indescribable gift
Our worship is a celebration of that gift

And of the giver
In our worship we have rediscovered
God's marvelous affirmation of life.

This is different from the faith
that many of us experienced in the past
Religion that was life-denying
Worship that was monochrome and one-dimensional
Where our senses and culture were left at the door.

Tonight we invite you to bring all that you are
into worship
Your struggles and failures,
Your joys and fears,
Your faith and your doubts.
Your culture,
Your sensuality,
Your whole self.

Bring your self and be at home now
God is here
And all are welcome.[1]

Bethlehem

Bethlehem is a place in our heads,
Some part of us assumes we could find our way through its dark streets,
After all we've known them since we were children.
And Bethlehem's sleep was deep and dreamless,

Or so we claim (as if we knew).
It's understandable that we claim too much
Because Bethlehem is a kind of toytown,
A place built of Duplo and fuzzy felt;
It is small and easily patronized, a little child of a place,
it could no more host the Millennium than the Olympics.

Bethlehem is a place in our heads,
Like Christmas it is intimately and uneasily linked to our sense of home.
And at Christmas some part of us needs to go there,
We need to go there because somehow in the history of our planet,
this obscure Middle Eastern town
Has become a symbol of the human home.

That is why all over the world tonight,
In Sydney and Delhi, in Lima and Lagos and London
People have built little Bethlehems in their churches and houses.

We bring Bethlehem home, because we sense that Bethlehem
stands for home, and not just simple sentimental home,
But an improvisation of home,
It stands for home in the face of homelessness,
and home in the face of God.[2]

God Waits

God waits for us,
not like a lion ready to pounce
if we let our guard down,
not like an interfering in-law
but like an old friend who's seen it all before
and likes us anyway,
with whom we can spend time
without having to pretend or explain.[3]

Waiting

As Sarah waited . . .
40 years for a son to fulfill God's promise
      We wait in hope for what we thought had been promised to us

As Moses waited . . .
40 years in the desert being prepared by God to lead his people
      We wait for emptiness and humility; for bravado to wither

As Israel waited . . .
40 years in the desert, hungry, depressed, thirsting, unsure
      We wait for things to move on and generations to pass

As the prophets waited . . .
1000 years of promises that God would raise up a Savior
      We wait for things to change

As Mary waited . . .
9 months of her 14 years for the child of God
      We feel the birth pangs yet fear for the child

As John the Baptist waited . . .
Scanning the crowds for the one whose sandals he would not be worthy
         to untie
      We long for an experience of the Divine

As Jesus waited . . .
30 years of creeping time
40 days in the desert of temptation
3 years in the midst of misunderstanding
3 days in the depths of hell
    So we wait for God's time
    Preparing the way
    Our turn to toil on leveling mountains and straightening paths
    Our turn to watch the time horizon
        Our turn to pass on the hope—
        the one who promised is faithful
        and will come back[1]

Light Meditation

How do you feel when the dark goes out?
Are you afraid of the light?
Does it make your eyes water?
Do you screw up your heart and hide under the covers?

The light is a flood that will level your landmarks to a plain,
leaving you no shelter or familiar territory.
It will carry away the house of your comfortable darkness
and give you only holy ground to stand on.
It will fall like stone upon you.
You will be the only thing that casts a shadow,
but your shadow will flee behind you where you cannot see it.

You will grope for definition like a climber in the fog,
your hands will search for edges that tell you what is and what is not,
and you will not find them.
You will cling to frozen certainty for fear of falling.
Your map will be too small.

The light will burn your skin.
The light will bleach your bones.
The light will leave you snow blind.
And you will not be the same.

You will look into the sun, and know the names of clouds.
You will learn 17 words for snow, and discern them all.
You will see the horizon, and not know how to come in.
You will forget how to talk, except too much and ecstatically.
Your speech will be oblique and without explanations.

And you will return to the darkness as a messenger
bearing an endless blazing sky within.[5]

The Starlit Darkness

[Give people time to follow this meditation, time to settle, and then time to
visualize—the pace should be gentle and unhurried, with plenty of pauses
in which people can imagine.]

- St. John of the Cross spoke of the dark night of the soul
- Karl Rahner said, "All clear understanding is grounded in the darkness
  of God"
- Helen Waddell describes Christianity as "the starlit darkness"
- Annie Dillard says: "You do not have to sit outside in the dark. If however
  you want to look at the stars you will find that darkness is required. The
  stars neither require it nor demand it."

We are going to take time to think about darkness in relation to God.
Take a few deep breaths to relax . . . and settle into a rhythm of steady breathing . . . Ask God to lead your imagination . . .

When you hear the word darkness what does it conjure up in your mind?

What images do you recall?
What places do you remember?
What feelings does it evoke in you?
What might it mean to speak of the darkness of God?

Just for a moment:
Imagine you are in a house in the country;
all the lights are on, artificial light, electric light.
It's time to leave;
You collect your coat and say your farewells and step outside.
It's not like the city—there are no streetlights.
As you step into the darkness everything goes pitch black.
You are dizzy with darkness,
You can't focus on anything.
You walk hesitantly down the path, feel for the gate and get through it.

Now you stand and wait and look around.

> Gradually what seemed pitch black becomes less so.
> Slowly, your eyes adjust—now you can make out the shapes of trees and
>   houses, and hills on the horizon.
> You feel the ground beneath your feet, solid and firm.
> You look up.
> Above you is the vast expanse of the heavens.
> What at first seemed to be only darkness you now see is starlit
> and incredibly beautiful.
> Galaxies, stars, planets, a crescent moon . . . this is the starlit darkness.
> The breathtaking darkness of God.
> The mystery of God.
> God is a starlit darkness—breathtaking . . .
> God is a starlit darkness.[6]

Logos

the meaning behind meaning
the word before words

tumbling into flesh
falling into flesh
slipping into flesh

logos spermatikos
logos ovatikos

embryonic born-again Eve–Adam

fused sperm–egg of godself
angeling itself in the soft angles of Mary's womb
decentering itself in the twisted gravity of creation
being fruitful and multiplying
spinning life into the genes of Jesus[7]

Matthew Says—Abraham Begat
(a genealogy of grace)

[Readers 1 and 2 should be men, reader 3 is a woman. This is a very de-
manding reading because of the names involved; in fact it is very rarely

read in church. To read it strongly and fluently in this way is very striking in itself—the commentary threaded through the text supplies what most hearers today will not automatically realize. This reading can be done well over music, the music should not be too slow or gentle, but should have a beat and an edge to it. The words should be read at a quick pace but not rushed.]

Reader 1:	This is the Genesis of Jesus Christ, the son of David, the son of Abraham
Reader 2:	Jesus' genealogy, his family tree, his pedigree, the time-line that claims him as King and Messiah, descended from the founders of the Jewish nation and their great kings
Reader 1:	This is the time-line from Abraham to David: Abraham, Isaac, Jacob, Perez
Reader 3:	*Perez' mother was Tamar, a wronged woman who made her own justice by conceiving a son with her father-in-law*
Reader 2:	Hezron, Aram, Aminadab, Nahshon, Salmon, Boaz—
Reader 3:	*Boaz' mother was Rahab, a prostitute who risked her life to protect Jewish fighters*
Reader 1:	and Obed . . .
Reader 3:	*His mother was Ruth, a foreigner, an outsider who married into the Jewish people*
Reader 2:	Jesse, King David
Reader 1:	This is the time-line from David to the exile: Solomon
Reader 3:	*His mother was Uriah's wife Bathsheba, a woman whose husband was murdered so that the king could marry her*
Reader 2:	Rehoboam, Abijah, Asaph, Jehoshaphat, Joram, Uzziah, Jotham, Ahaz, Hezekiah, Manasseh, Amos, Josiah, Jechoniah—he was deported into Babylon
Reader 1:	This is the time-line from the exile to the birth of Jesus: Salathiel, Zerubbabel, Abiud, Eliakim, Azor, Zadok, Achim, Eliud, Eleazar, Matthan, Jacob, Joseph

Reader 3:   *His wife was Mary, a young betrothed woman who became*
pregnant before her marriage

Reader 1:   Matthew says this history has a shape
Matthew tells it as God's story
Matthew suggests our story links back to this story,
If these are also our roots . . .

Reader 2:   Abraham is our father, Sarah our mother
David is our king,

Reader 3:   This is our family tree, a tree with many roots,
A closet full of skeletons
A story of incest, prostitution and mixed parentage
This is no genealogy of purity or pride,
this is a genealogy of grace

. . .

Reader 1:   As a sign of our connection with the past, we are going to
write our own time-line, a line which carries the names we
know of the generations above us, the generation of those
who like Mary were our birth parents, or like Joseph were
our carers.

Reader 2:   We, like Jesus, are all born into a family tree with its own
history of shame and defiance, of glory and exile, we
like Jesus are all born into an ethnically mixed line of
descent, we too are the children of hope and longing and
defeat.

Reader 3:   As we trace our own line, we look not for purity, but for
grace. Matthew's genealogy says the Messiah is birthed out
of longing, out of the pain of our history, out of the pain of
women, out of the longing for freedom, out of a sense of
urgency, out of our need to be saved.

   To us and to our time, we pray: Come, Emmanuel—
come to your people, come and set us free.[8]

Matthew Says— Hail Joseph
(a kind of dream sequence)

[This reading can be done with one voice but is best with three. One (female?) reads the Scripture passage, a man reads the Joseph voice, and a woman reads the final Hail Joseph. In a men only group, the final reading is also very moving when done by a man.]

Reader 1   Reading: Matthew 1:18–20a
Reader 2   Hail Joseph, passed over among men,
Generations shall rise and say: "Who is he?"

But listen—I have a history, a family, a name,
All I wanted, is what most men want,
to take my place, to play my part . . .
Not such a vanity, I don't think,
just what any man might ask,
That my children would recite my name in the genealogy,
That when they told the story they would tell my part,
When they gave thanks—it would also be for me!

I hardly knew Mary, she was young and I was older
The way things were we didn't mix much;
She was shy at the ceremony—shy and veiled;

When they told me, I didn't shout and scream,
I didn't want to kick the dust up into a great cloud of shame,
It just wasn't what I felt,
I felt only that tremendous weariness a man feels when something good
has been lost, a sadness too deep for tears, a wound too deep for words;
I felt a need to turn within myself, a need to hide,
I longed for the nights and the soft, sweet oblivion of sleep.

It was at night, the angel spoke to me,
All fire and feathers, like an angel should be, beautiful and wild, and strong;

She said: Joseph, the child is God's;
don't be afraid, Joseph; the child is a Holy Ghost child;
don't be ashamed, don't be afraid!
(She looked like one of Mary's friends)

So when you sing the names, my name should not be there,
Or should it be?
Should I not stand with childless Abraham
and with all these fathers of the nation,

all of whom were impotent to kindle life sometimes
But unlike them, the power of the promise didn't flow out
through my veins,
or through my sex,
I am the man God set aside, the man God did not need to light this light,
the man God could not use to fire this fuse,
(I didn't even get to choose the name)
I lost all this, I lost my place in time and this instead,
this unsought gift which comes not through my loins,
but through my hands and heart and head,
This comes instead—the power to care and raise this boy-child
up to be a different kind of man . . .
And be a different man myself . . .

[woman's voice]
Hail Joseph, blessed among men.

. . .

Let this same mind be in you which was also in Joseph,
Who did not think equality with God something to be snatched at,
But humbled himself, taking the form of a carer,
He was obedient before the gift of life,
Even life given without the help of a man . . .

Hail Joseph, Godfather of God.[9]

The Great Reversal

Walking with the crowds,
Carried along by the pressing forward.
Each one eager to get ahead,
but each one starting the same—born as a baby and from then on
struggling towards meaning, power and influence.
Be someone,
Be remembered,
Make a big impression;
leave some indelible mark in your 3 score years and 10.

From birth, a struggle to find eternity, to burst through life
with such dazzling intensity that everyone will remember forever.
But walking the other way, pick out a route against the crowds,
a solitary figure passes me, passes all of us—all straining
away innocence, to be someone and he passes us, a quiet chaos in the crowd.

Christ, eternal, omniscient, creator, beyond time, source of
wisdom, and beyond petty claims of influence . . . in very nature
God, slips into reverse and walks back past us—away from
Kingship, away from power, away from influence, away from
eternity, away from wisdom, towards infancy,
Calmly stepping into the body of a tiny child.

And even as this baby grows, figuring out how to control the
body he himself designed, he still walks the other way,
realizing that life cannot be found in the struggle for
permanence, but in giving it up.

The great reversal subverts me. Tired of pressing forward, I
realize I need to turn, for what I have been searching for has
just walked past me the other way.

Prayer

Infinite God we have struggled to make our marks on this world
We confess that this has often led to trampling on others;
rushing for seats on the train; pushing in front; me first

Infant God teach us about the great reversal; lead us into selfless-
ness. In this city straining towards success help us to live
a different way in the simple things: courtesy, honesty, humility.

Crucified God in the bread we remember your body broken,
given up so that we might live. In eating it we commit to the
way of sacrifice. In the wine we remember your blood shed,
poured out to reverse our wrong doings. In drinking it we
commit to the way of forgiveness.
Amen.[10]

Come and Be Born in Us

Jesus of Bethlehem and Nazareth and Calvary,
We are expecting you tonight.
Come and be born in us.

Jesus of the manger and the inn,
Jesus of the workshop and the temple,
Jesus of the lakeside and the city,
Jesus of the fireside and the roadside,
We are expecting you tonight.
Come and be born in us.

Jesus of Mary and Joseph,
Jesus of shepherds and angels,
Jesus of children and animals,
Jesus of fishermen and priests,
Jesus of women and men disciples,
Jesus of tax collectors and prostitutes,
Jesus of all who will receive you,
We are expecting you tonight.
Come and be born in us.

Look and see,
We have brought our bread and wine
To be your body for us.

[bring in the bread and the wine]

Look and see,
We have brought our flesh and blood,
To be your body for you.
Look and see,
The same Spirit which lived in your flesh
Is *living* in your people here.

Look at us and let us look at you
And see you now.

We are expecting you tonight.
Come and be born in us.[11]

Christmas Communion Thanksgiving

We give thanks to you living God,
For your creation which lies in us and around us,
By the power of your Spirit you made the universe,
By the strength of your Word you gave us life,
The holy angels sang for joy when you made earth and heaven.

We give thanks to you, loving God,
For your liberation which is with us and near us,
By the power of your Spirit Jesus was born of Mary,
By the weakness of his flesh you have redeemed the world,
The holy angels sang for joy when he was born.

It is our duty and our joy,
To sing with your people of all places and times,

To worship you and proclaim your praise
With all of heaven's angels and to share their song.

Sanctus

Prayer of Consecration

Words at Distribution

Jesus Christ is here for you
Draw near with faith
Let Christ be born in you and you in Christ

[as people receive]

Let Christ be born in you and you in Christ[12]

The Sign Communion — We Bring Gifts

Out of the richness of the world and from its poverty
We bring gifts to God, the Creator

We bring bread — Thank you our God for bread
For a harvest which did not fail
For hands which worked it and money to buy it
We bring bread to make the sign for body

We bring wine — Thank you our God for wine
For vines which grew and bore fruit
For hands which made it and money to buy it
We bring wine to make the sign for blood

We bring ourselves — Thank you our God for life
For the work of creation trusted to women and men
For bodies which shaped and carried our bodies
We bring ourselves to make the sign for love

On the night he was betrayed, Jesus Christ gave his disciples a sign
Use this sign to remember me he said
Broken bread and poured out wine

People of God, this is your sign
Christ is here in bread and wine[13]

We Believe in One God

We believe in One God
The Eternal Power of Life and Goodness
The Maker of Space and Time
Who was and is and is to come

We believe in God our Maker
Whose love fires the sun
Whose word made the world
Whose law is the good

We believe in Jesus Christ,
Child of God and Mary's Child,
Born into Palestine,
A prophet of Israel.
Born in a stable,
A victim of Empire.
Born to a woman
And made in her image.
Born of the Spirit
The icon of God.
Born as a savior
Of sinners and victims.
Born as a healer
Of wounds and diseases.
Born as a teacher
Of wisdom and justice.

We believe in the Holy Spirit
The intimacy of God with creation
The power of God against death
Whose breath lives in all life
Whose peace gathers the church
Whose love sends God's people in mission.

We believe in one God,
Our Maker, Savior and Helper
A trinity of Beauty and Holiness
A community of joy,
To this holy and awesome God
We give glory and praise,
Now and forever, Amen.[14]

I Believe in God

I believe in God,
Three in one
Father, Son, Spirit
Paradox
Mystery
Elemental

I believe in a God of Justice,
Compassion, mercy, hope
And first, a God of love
Love personified, incarnated

I believe in God,
the mother of Creation
God, the father of humanity
God, the lover of us all

I believe we are called:
To activity out of passivity and apathy,
By the Son of God, through his actions
Calling down through history,
Borne on the wings of the Spirit

I believe we are called:
To community, with each other
Through Christ the thread
Weaving us all together

I believe that God plays no favorites
Pulls no punches
Leaves no stone unturned

I believe that life is hard
I believe that life is beautiful
So, I believe, does God[15]

Adventure of Reality

Eternal God
born into one place and time for the sake of every place and time,
wherever we live you are already there
waiting to be discovered in the adventure of reality,
give us discernment to follow your tracks
through the cutting edge of culture and the voices of our times.

Make us bold to step outside our old religious comforts,
to live and build your kingdom with the stuff that's all around us.[16]

The Sign

We could tell you the story, God . . .
And there were in the same country
shepherds keeping watch in the fields
And angels sang to them
A song about a sign.

We could say it was

An insignificant sign
Bad advertising
The Logos had no recognizable logo
A scruffy piece of presentation

And shepherds looked on
Like we do again this year.

This is your sign—the angels said
What's ours God?
Is it the same—Even now?

And what happened to those shepherds?
Did it mark them? Your sign . . .

All the book says is
They went home worshiping.

We could do worse.

God of heaven and earth, committed to the ones
Who faded out of the story
Commit to us after all this thinking goes quiet
And lend your glory to the rest of our time.
Through Jesus Christ, our Lord, Amen.[17]

Sleeping Bag

Jesus is in the sleeping bag
stopping over
he comes round any time he likes
right time, wrong time
he don't mind

foxes have holes birds have nests
but the son of man has the sofa

he's poking round the fridge
which needs defrosting
old sins stuck in the icebox
fruit gone bad
leftovers still left over
he throws them out
I guess I should clean up but I never get much warning
it's embarrassing
but I'd still rather he came

we sit up late talking
where we've been
and where we're going next
he's already bought the tickets
all I have to do is take the time off work
new sneakers on the floor
goodnight rustle in the corner
the room feels warmer
with him in it[18]

Rituals

CANDLE LIGHTING

Description

Lighting a candle as we pray is one of the oldest rituals known to us in the church. It is also a common heartfelt response from people everywhere in situations of grief or trouble to light candles as a vigil in memory, prayer, or solidarity (for example after the death of Princess Diana in the UK and after the destruction of the World Trade Center in the USA). There are probably a thousand different ways to use candles in prayer.

Items needed

Candles, tapers for lighting, matches, possibly sand tray to stand candles in.

Instructions for setting up

Have the unlit candle(s) set up and some matches and a taper nearby. In the case of using small candles have one candle lit and others nearby. Ask people to light their candle from one that is already lit.

A candle with three wicks can be lit at the start of the service to symbolize the presence of the Trinity. As each wick is lit a prayer relating to that person of the Trinity is said.

People can be invited to light a candle to take away with them to symbolize taking the light of Christ with them back to their own situations.

A sand tray with small candles or night lights can be set up at a station and people invited to go and light a candle to pray for somebody they know or a particular situation in the world. A variation on this is to have a map of the world and people can place the night light on the part of the world they wish to pray for.

Other ideas

A contemporary take on candle lighting is to set up a laptop computer and light some virtual candles such as those produced on www.embody.co.uk in the "sanctuary." These are lit by clicking on the candle with the mouse.

Project images of candles or flames on screens around the worship space. Perhaps the easiest homemade video loop is of a candle burning. Projected on screens or televisions around the worship space this can look stunning.[19]

DARKNESS AND LIGHT

Items needed

Glow-in-the dark stars, potting soil, a large flat piece of wood about the size of a table top, a bright light.

Instructions for setting up

In the middle of the worship space cover a large surface in soil. This could be on a tabletop, an old door, or large piece of wood. Scatter some glow-in-the-dark stars on top of the soil. Also set up a very bright light ready to dazzle the main worship space.

Description

Have the lights off or very low and read the meditation on "The Starlit Darkness" (pages 38–39). Soil is very absorbent of light and looks incredibly dark in a lowlit environment. People should be seated around the soil so that it is a focus for the meditation.

Then—unannounced—turn the lights on as brightly as possible and read the "Light Meditation" (pages 37–38).

Then turn the bright lights off again and the glow-in-the-dark stars should glow brightly in the soil—the starlit darkness.

Other ideas

An alt way of using the two pieces would be to have them in separate rooms. You could use a sensor light for the light room. This room could be set up very dark. When people walked into it the light came on. The "Light Meditation" could be printed for people to read. When they left, the light would go out again. But you would have to instruct people to do it one at a time otherwise the effect would be lost.

Project an image of a starry night sky onto the ceiling of the building when the lights are turned off to reveal the glow-in-the-dark stars.[20]

INCENSE

Items needed

Incense (usually available from Catholic bookshops); a thurible, or a portable grill placed on a concrete slab; a fire extinguisher.

Instructions for setting up

If you have access to a proper incense burner (a thurible) you will need some pieces of charcoal and get them burning several minutes before you wish to use the thurible so that the charcoal is hot when you place the incense on it and swing it. If you use a portable grill, if you are inside you need to make sure that your setup is safe. One way of doing this is to make sure that the grill is raised off the ground and the legs of the grill are on concrete paving slabs rather than the carpet. The charcoal will need to be lit perhaps half an hour before you wish to use it in the service so that you just have hot coals rather than flames. Have a fire extinguisher adjacent to the grill and someone to stand by the grill at all times to make sure no one (especially younger children) goes too near it. Place the incense in a bowl by the grill.

Description

Incense was used in the worship of the Jerusalem temple as a sign of the prayers and praise of God's people ascending to heaven. It is referred to in the book of Revelation as a symbol of prayer and praise. Orthodox, Roman Catholic, and High Church traditions use incense in their worship as a symbol of the purifying presence of God and of the prayers of the church ascending to God.

Burning incense to accompany prayers adds a dimension of otherness and mystery. If using the thurible, ask the person to walk around among the people swinging it during prayers. If using the grill, invite people to come forward and to place one or two pieces/granules of incense on the barbecue as a way of offering their prayer to God.

Other ideas

This is a great way to end an evening where an actual barbecue has been held outside or a campfire.

A video of incense burning is also a good accompaniment to prayers.[21]

WAILING WALL

Items needed

A convenient nearby brick wall or one that you construct from square prayer kneelers or something equivalent in a church; pens and pieces of paper or Post-it notes.

Instructions for setting up

Put pens and paper in front of the wall you intend to use. If there are gaps/holes in it prayers can be posted in those. Otherwise they can be stuck on the wall with Blu-Tack or an equivalent. If you are making a wall, it is a good idea to do it against a wall of the building so that it doesn't topple over. The good thing about making one from prayer kneelers, say, is that it has gaps in it in which prayers can be posted.

Description

The wailing wall in Jerusalem is a site for pilgrimage and prayer. (It is not an uncontroversial one as it is actually built on land that was originally the homes of Palestinians that were subsequently destroyed.) This prayer ritual involves people writing prayers on pieces of paper and rolling them up and placing them in cracks in the wall (if there aren't cracks in the wall, use Post-it notes or Blu-Tack to stick the prayers to the wall). The focus of the prayers is ideally one of lament, or it could be on intercession for walls of alienation to be broken down.

Other ideas

This could be used outdoors against a wall that symbolizes alienation in the community in some way.[22]

WALKING A LABYRINTH

Items needed

Lots of masking tape or duct tape to mark out the labyrinth path; items/
readings/reflections to place on the path as required.

Instructions for setting up

You can lay out a labyrinth using tape on either a floor, a carpet, or a piece
of cloth. The designs with straight lines are simpler to tape out. The designs
with a circular pattern might take more time or be better painted onto a large
piece of cloth. It takes a considerable amount of time to lay them out, so allow
several hours to set up.

Description

Labyrinths were a feature of many medieval cathedrals—one of the best
remaining examples is found in Chartres Cathedral in northern France. Unlike a maze they have only one path—there are no dead-ends. People walk
the labyrinth slowly, as an aid to contemplative prayer and reflection, as a
spiritual exercise, or as a form of pilgrimage.

Walking a labyrinth is an absorbing and deeply involving ritual.

Most labyrinths have three stages to the journey: the inward journey which
is a time of letting go or shedding, and preparation to meet with God; the
central space where the walker lingers to spend time in prayer with God; and
the outward journey where the walker takes his or her encounter with God
back with them into the world.

There are a whole range of labyrinth designs, and you can come up with
your own. And there are lots of ways to use this simple ritual.

It can be a walk for people to make at their own pace to use as an aid to
prayer and meditation.

You can add to it by playing quiet music in the background to create a mood.
At intervals, Scriptures or meditations relating to the themes of incarnation,
journey, letting go, focusing on God, could be read out as people walk. This
way before and after people get their turn to walk the labyrinth they can sit
around it and there is something for them to focus on.

You can also add things on to the path—things to read, or rituals to do.
Some designs have a number of stopping-points on the journey that are de-
liberately wider spaces so that they can incorporate these things. "Letting
go," "distractions," and "impressions" are examples of the kinds of rituals
you could include.

A labyrinth design and the accompanying stations and meditations can be found in detail on the website www.labyrinth.org.uk. The meditations on this were originally recorded on a CD. The walker put on a CD Discman and listened to the appropriate track at each stopping-point.

Other ideas

Set up a labyrinth outside—on a beach or in a park or at a festival.

Visit the virtual labyrinth. Go to www.labyrinth.org.uk, click on "do it," and experience the uniqueness of the labyrinth online.[23]

CHRIST PRESENT IN CULTURE

Items required

A table, candles, a cross, items that are the stuff of popular culture (Play-station, magazines, CDs, etc.), a large image of an icon of Christ, a CD of Gregorian chants, or something similar.

Instructions for setting up

Set up a table at the front or in the middle of the worship space, but as well as the usual things that might go on it (a cross, a Bible, candles, bread and wine) place items there that represent the world/culture of the people at the service. These might be artifacts of popular culture (magazines, CDs, a computer, etc.).

Description

Many traditions use processions as part of their worship. This ritual is a reworking of that simple idea.

For the procession play some appropriate music (something overtly religious like a Gregorian chant could work well, or you could use an instrumental piece such as "Alright Climbatise" by The Prodigy). Have everyone stand and some people process in slowly with some large candles and an icon of Christ. If you have access to a thurible (swinging incense burner), that would also add to the drama. The icon could be contemporary or traditional. The candles are placed on the table, and the icon of Christ is placed in the middle of the stuff to symbolize Christ coming in the midst of culture. This could accompany readings on the incarnation and could be concluded with the prayer "Adventure of Reality" (pages 48–49).

Other ideas

You could invite people to bring the items with them and build the table as an earlier part of the service.[24]

ICONS OF THE PRESENT

Items needed

None

Instructions for setting up

Set up a table or cloth in the center of the worship space. Place one or two candles and maybe a traditional icon or a cross there to convey the sense of it being a sacred space.

Description

An icon is a window on eternity, something that when we look at it enables us to see beyond it and through it to God. Traditional icons can be very inspiring, but lots of people have other things from contemporary culture that function in this way in their lives. As part of a service have a discussion on what those things might be. Maybe a picture, a piece of music, an object, standing on the seashore or watching the sunset, a space in the city. Then invite people to bring an "icon of the present" to the next service (or something that represents it if it is impossible to bring). Have them bring and place these things on a table in the center or at the front of the worship space, and give a word of explanation if they'd like to. These could be accompanied by more traditional icons or placed on the table with bread and wine as part of a communion service.

Other ideas

There may be items that people bring that are able to be incorporated into other worship services (music items, images, etc.). It would be a good idea to at least take some photographs of these icons of the present so that they can be projected round the worship space on future occasions.[25]

THE RABBIT HOLE

Items needed

Some red and blue "pills" — jelly beans are ideal. Loud dance music. *The Matrix* video.

Instructions for setting up

If you have a packet of mixed jelly beans sort out the red and the blue ones. Depending on how you want to do the ritual, either place them all on an offertory plate to be passed around or place a red and a blue jelly bean in a small bag for everyone to have one bag each.

Description

This ritual connects with the film *The Matrix*. It may make sense to show the appropriate clip from the film as part of the service or have the connection explained. The plot of the film is that machines have taken over the world. Humans are being used as batteries for machines, but they are wired up so that in their minds they experience living in the world. What appears to be the real world is nothing more than an illusion, a computer simulation. There is a scene in the film where the character Neo is offered the chance to discover this truth for himself. To do so he is offered the choice of swallowing a red pill or a blue pill. If he takes the blue pill, he will wake up in his bed and continue in the illusion, comfortably numb to the truth. If he takes the red pill he will discover the truth but also the risky adventure that goes with it. The metaphor of Alice in Wonderland is used where she tumbles down the rabbit hole — "You take the red pill and I show you how deep the rabbit hole goes."

In response to a challenge (following Christ or following his example in mission, say) invite people to take either a red or a blue jelly bean — the red to signify taking the risk of following Christ, the blue to signify forgetting the challenge. These could be passed round on an offertory plate, they could be part of a station that people visit, or they could be given out at the end for people to take away and reflect on their response. In the latter case it would be good to prepare small bags with a red and blue jelly bean in each. This ritual seems to work best accompanied by loud dance music.

Other ideas

You could loop the video clip from the film so that it keeps playing during the ritual and the rest of the service.

You could sample the spoken portion of the film where Morpheus says "Take the red pill . . ." and mix it in with a loud dance track.

If using the ritual as a challenge to engage in mission with contemporary culture rather than staying in the safe confines of the Christian subculture or church, the prayer "Adventure of Reality" (pages 48–49) would be a good conclusion to the ritual.[26]

GREAT REVERSAL

Items needed

None

Instructions for setting up

You need a space wide enough for people to stand across in a single line.

Description

Ask everyone to line up across the church facing the rear, to be asked a series of questions. If they answer yes, they step forward; if they answer no, they take a step back; if they are unsure or unwilling to make a statement, they remain where they are. The questions begin. "Have you had a vacation this year? Do you have a loving family? Do you have a rewarding love life? Do you feel you have a special gift?" And so on. By the end, after about 10 questions, the line has become a spread pattern of spiritual states, the fortunate out in front, the less fortunate left behind. And now the coup. Ask everybody to turn around to face the altar. For God has decreed the great reversal—and suddenly, the fortunate first are at the back, and the last are out in front.

List of possible questions

Have you had a vacation this year?

Do you have a loving family?

Do you feel you have a special gift?

Do you feel close to God?

Have you plenty of food in your kitchen?

Do you know your neighbors?

Is your car less than five years old?

Do you have someone to share your secrets with?

Do you feel valued at work?
Do you get enough rest?
Do you own your home?
Are you at peace with all your friends?
Do you have a rewarding love life?
Do you give something up for Lent?
Are you at peace with yourself?
Have you seen something beautiful recently?
Are you financially secure?
Do you have good memories of childhood?
Do you have good health?
Has anyone ever bought you flowers?

Other ideas

This accompanies the reading "The Great Reversal" (pages 43–44).
Use accompanying video images of everything going backwards—people
walking; traffic; and so on.[27]

Ritual

Every teacher of the law who has been instructed about the kingdom of heaven is like the owner of a house who brings out of his storeroom new treasures as well as old.

Matthew 13:52 NIV

In many low church traditions, "ritual" is a dirty word. Talk of ritual or of being ritualistic has long been a way of condemning church practice, either as superstitious or as quenching the freedom of the Spirit.

The alt worship movement has been marked by a turn towards ritual, and there are some signs that this turn has already had ripples of influence across the charismatic and evangelical traditions. This embrace of ritual values it as a resource with real quality, depth, and richness in our current cultural situation in the West.

WHAT IS RITUAL FOR?

We believe the intention of ritual in liturgy is to facilitate encounter with God by choreographing a community's sensory experience in ways which intensify their ability to attend to particular dimensions of worship.

Again and again in Grace, we have found that God meets us in ritual so we nearly always try to incorporate some sort of ritual that everybody can be involved in. Doing an activity in response to God with others opens up a window in our souls and our community through which the breeze of the Spirit can blow. It

draws a service together and seals what has taken place. It moves worship from
our heads to our hearts.[28]

There is something of a mystery surrounding how this works in practice, but it
is transforming—often in powerful ways.

We find that ritual is best made open to everybody. The kind of response
where only a few people take part can leave others feeling excluded or second
best. Ritual also works on a variety of levels and often all ages can engage in
it—we have found that children in our communities particularly look forward
to "the doing bits!"

There is nothing new about using ritual in worship, but in some cases old
rituals have been allowed to dry up and lose their meaning. Our experience has
been that taking them on and reinventing them, playing with them, making
connections with contemporary life, reinvesting them with meaning, is very
exciting. They come alive in unprecedented ways.

Of course some traditions will ask what the fuss is about. They have never
lost or left ritual in their worship. We offer our respect and gratitude to them
for the gifts they have been stewards of, but we also believe that ritual is being
rediscovered in a new context in alt worship. We know from experience that some
traditions which prize ritual will shudder at the innovations in the ritual practice
of emerging churches and we freely admit that the intense interest of alt worship
groups in ritual does not often extend to the tight liturgical codes of many high
church practitioners. We use ritual in eclectic ways, often discarding or revising
elements which seem irrelevant or unhelpful. The roles of priests and clergy are
often decentered and shared out between multiple bodies and voices. We have
also created many new rituals, some of which have been tacky and unrepeatable,
others of which have been coherent, awe-inspiring, and powerful.

Some Protestant traditions have rejected rituals because of theological
anxieties about them. They have not been prepared to embrace the project
of "reforming ritual" and have ended up throwing the baby out with the Holy
Water. Western churches with strong traditions of using ritual still often fail to
see that their ritual practice has been shaped by local culture and custom before
being freeze-dried at one stage of its development. (Our advice is to feel free to
rehydrate from a local water supply.)

Communion, baptism, the imposition of ashes, the laying on of hands,
anointing with oil, lighting candles or burning incense to pray, footwashing,
walking a labyrinth, the stations of the cross—these are all examples of old rituals still rich with meaning. Guidelines for enacting both old and new rituals are
included throughout the book in the hope that you will appreciate the sources
and roots of ritual in the life of the churches, but also sense a freedom to make
them your own.

Not by Prose Alone

Theology is sometimes called "Godtalk." Worship embodies styles and habits of talking about and to God. The nature of this speech or the tone of language is vitally important. Some critics of church tradition argue that our capacity for speech has been vastly reduced in the modern era. The poet Les Murray contrasts the terms "narrowspeak" and "wholespeak" to illustrate his thinking on ways of talking about God.[29] He suggests that in recent times (modernity) Godtalk has been severely reduced to narrowspeak, the voice of reason—rational and didactic ways of talking, the discourse of prose. Narrowspeak has to "make sense," be explainable, and be easily understood by everyone. It is communication reduced to just words, words, and more words.

Wholespeak in contrast is a poetic discourse, mystical speech, a language which is "truly dreamed." This is very similar to Walter Brueggemann's appeal to the church to rediscover poetry rather than living by prose alone. Both Murray and Brueggemann argue that the church needs to rediscover wholespeak or poetry, rather than feeling obliged to adopt the language of modernity. We might call this the re-enchantment or re-mythologization of speech, where speech reflects the Christian imagination, recognizing the importance of symbols, images, "myths," and metaphors as well as sharing space and time with music and the visual arts. Truth can be carried or opened up just as effectively (or maybe better) by this kind of language.

The Eternal Word Had a Northern Accent

Wholespeak involves more than a positive attitude towards poetic language; it also affirms a diversity of accents and dialects. Much of the official liturgy of the main denominations can feel as though it ought to be read in standard English, as it often has been in recent history. We need to shift the tone and feel of liturgy away from this kind of social elitism. We can still value form, without clinging to formality. We want language to be powerful, well crafted, and apt for the moment, but that can come from "customized" language just as much as from standardized English.

Alt worship is often associated with musical styles or visual images, but it has also been concerned with looking again at how language is used in worship.

The Message translation of the New Testament[30] was striking because it radically broke with the formality of more traditional translations and opted for a more poetic and dynamic "free" translation style. Some bits work better than others, but it has been an important resource for alt worship groups as they work on the language of their services.

If we can move towards wholespeak in worship, we believe the language of worship will become richer, edgier, more poetic, and allusive. It will become more comic and satirical, but also more beautiful and more political. It will become less like CNN English and more accented. It will become less like official service books and more like the Bible—and that will be a good thing.

Part 2

Lent

Resources

Long distrusted by low-church Protestants, the season of Lent is becoming ever more widely accepted. More and more corners of the church now seem able to embrace it as an opportunity rather than a threat.

The word Lent in English comes from the word for Spring. The season owes its origins to the practice of preparing candidates for baptism at Easter. Over time, this special period of preparation evolved into a spiritual discipline offered to all believers as they prepared for the great festivals of Holy Week and Easter.

Lent makes more sense when it is begun seriously on Ash Wednesday. The ritual of anointing with ash has traditionally been observed mainly by Roman and Anglo-Catholics but has been widely taken up by alt worship groups and is increasingly seen in unprecedented corners of US churches.

The spiritual journey of Lent is not presented as an easy one. The great themes of Lent represent areas of struggle and vulnerability for all believers—mortality and death, temptation and resistance, repentance and holiness. The classic location of this struggle is the desert or wilderness, the place of wandering, waiting, hunger, and temptation.

Lent is a time when many people will practice the discipline of fasting, for shorter or longer periods of time. Bodies incarnate the spiritual detox.

Against those who label Lent as pathological guilt-raking, the Taizé Book of Common Prayer has described these forty days as "a celebration of the joy of God's forgiveness."

Into the Desert

Then Jesus was led up by the Spirit into the wilderness to be tempted by the devil. (Matthew 4:1)

The LORD says about his people:

"I am going to lure her and lead her out into the wilderness and speak to her heart." (Hosea 2:14)

Jesus says: "When you pray, go into your room and shut the door and pray to your Father who is in secret; and your Father who sees in secret will reward you." (Matthew 6:6)

Not every desert in our lives is one we are led into by God, and not all the time we spend wandering in the wilderness is time given to God.

But God does lead people into the desert, not to punish them, but as an act of love. Hosea tells us that God "lures" the people, God "woos" us away from a thousand other things that are making a claim on us and leads us jealously to a place in which we can be alone with God our Lover.

The desert is not a place of escape. If the desert we are in is a place of trouble in our lives then it is obviously not so. Even if we choose to spend time away in the desert it is not to escape just as the monastery is not an escape from the world.

The wise monk Thomas Merton said that we must only leave the world to learn to love it more. We must only leave behind needy people in order to become more committed to serving them. We must only embrace celibacy in order to deepen our love for men or women and ourselves. We must only vow poverty as a way of learning to see true value in the world. We must only waste time with God as a way of discovering what the time of our lives is for.

The desert is not a place for self-hatred or masochism. The Holy Spirit leads us into the desert to speak to our hearts.

To go into the desert is to go on a journey of the heart.[1]

An Approach to God—Losing My Religion

To some, God is the transcendent power waiting for us in everything
To others, God is an oppressive power used to bind and blind the wretched of the earth

To some, God is the creator who breathes the breath of life into our bodies
To others, God is the creation of an infantile humanity, superstitious and scared to grow up

To some, God is a motherly parent, birthing creation and holding her people to her breast

To others, God is a tyrannical father, never pleased enough, loathed and
feared as he traps us in dependence

To some, God is a liberator, hearing the cries of the oppressed and moving to
help them
To others, God is a collaborator, deaf to the cries of the oppressed and sid-
ing with the powers that be

To some God's hands were split open by violence in suffering love for
women and men
To others God's hands are stained with the blood of countless atrocities
and needless human suffering

To some, the praises of the church rise like incense to be breathed in by the
God of love
To others, the smoke of Auschwitz and Hiroshima rises like a finger ac-
cusing God, like smoke which blinds God's eyes

Some of us find all our hope and sense of meaning in God
Others have lost all faith in God

God means something to us,
to our worship or our doubt,
to our trust or our fear,
as lover or as tyrant,
as ultimate reality or grand illusion.
We are here to face up to what we do and don't believe about God.

Let us worship God.[2]

Prodigal Returns

It was while we were yet far off
Before we had hatched a plan
or mapped a route back to your heart.
Before we had sent a postcard
to warn you of our imminent return.
While we were yet far off
you could see our footprints
turning in the opposite direction.
You knew that our hearts were entirely captured
before ever we recognized
a chink in our self-centered armor.
While we were yet far off
You had sent out the invitations

and blown up the balloons.
The presents were wrapped
and the chairs pushed back
to make room for the dancing.
As we rounded the corner
we could dimly see you,
craning your neck and leaping for joy.
We thought then
that a reconciliation might be possible;
While we were yet far off
you popped the cork
and added the final touches
to the party tea.[3]

Prodigal's Brother

Why do I feel so bad, heavy hearted, sad inside?
Why at a time of celebration am I bitter—unable to join in?
Why do I feel neglected, unwanted, unloved, uncelebrated?

I'm supposed to open my arms too, without judging
I'm supposed to forgive, without entertaining thoughts of punishment or
    justice
I'm not sure I'm ready for this—it will take time
I'm not sure I'm big enough for this—it will take more love than I feel

"He was lost and has been found" I'm told
"Come celebrate and rejoice" I'm invited
"All that I have is yours" I'm promised
"He's your brother" I'm reminded.[4]

Prodigal Confession

WE CONFESS THE SINS OF THE YOUNGER SON

We confess that we take all you have to give while denying that you were ever
    our father.
We confess that we hoped you were dead.
We confess that we declared ourselves masters of our own destiny, free
    from the superstitious rules of humanity's childhood; and now find that
    we have only ourselves to blame for things that go wrong.
We confess that we prefer the identities we can buy, wear, and discard
    to the vulnerable robes of sonship and daughterhood.
We confess that we paint our faces and neglect our souls.
We confess that we are willing victims of those who tell us who to be
    because it is in their financial interest to do so.

We confess that we are in rags in the pigsty, trying to remember who we once thought we were.
We confess our emptiness; our inability to live on what the system gives us, or to be the machine that the system wants us to be.
We confess that we are to others the system that does not feed; we are to others the system that dehumanizes.
We confess that what we find unbearable when it is asked of us, is what we ask of others.

WE CONFESS THE SINS OF THE OLDER SON

We confess that we do our duty while hiding our resentment, saying thank you with our lips while saying "is that it?" in our thoughts.
We confess that we insist on our rights rather than waiting for your gifts.
We confess that we judge the younger son harshly and pride ourselves on our superiority; forgetting that pride is the deadliest sin.
We confess that we think it rather weak of you to welcome and forgive so readily; we wish you would live up to our moral standards.
We confess that we do in our hearts what the younger son did in a foreign country; our hearts have become a foreign country to you.

We ask to be forgiven and to be helped to live new lives, both those who went away and those who stayed but went away in their hearts. We want to return home to your embracing welcome, and celebrate with you the feast for a son who was dead and is alive again.[5]

Impression

In front of you is some sand
You remove your socks and shoes
Tread in the sand to leave your footprints
Step back and look at them
Where you have walked has left an impression

What will be left of us when we've left
when we're gone under down into darkness, the earth and memory?
When our dust and ashes have shaken themselves down and reverted to their original state
will their miraculous interlude have leaned on history's rudder?

What will be left of us when we've left?
What traces will we leave?
Will the evidence be compelling?
What will the surviving witnesses say?
How will they know we were here?

Will the future be better because of what we did with our present?

How many breaths make a life?
How long does it take to make a difference? (When can I start?)
What will history say of us when we're history too?

What will be left of us when we've left?[6]

Arable Parable

A farmer went out to sow his seed.
As he was scattering the seed, some fell along the path
and the birds ate it up.

Maybe you've been on this path so long that it's the only way ahead you can
    see.

So busy you couldn't keep track of the journey.
Maybe you looked up one day to realize you'd come further than you
    thought down this track.
Maybe the things that happened to you along the way have only hardened
    your heart further.
Perhaps you have become, along the way, impenetrable.

A farmer went out to sow his seed.
Some fell on rocks and stones where it didn't have much soil.
It sprang up quickly because the soil was shallow,
but when the sun came up the plants were scorched and they withered because
    they had no roots.

It isn't hard to feel rootless in this fast changing world.
People and places come and go, relationships shift and change.
Security and permanence are often an elusive quarry.
And eventually you give less deeply, engage less enthusiastically.
Enjoyment becomes short lived:
Nothing satisfies, nothing offers substance.
You'd put down roots if only you knew where to begin.

A farmer went out to sow his seed.
Some fell among thorns which grew up and choked the plants.

It's easy to become distracted;
Our culture conspires to suck us in to the feeding frenzy of wanting and hav-
    ing and wanting more.
Stop

Stand back
What do you really need?

A farmer went out to sow his seed.
And some fell on the good soil where it produced a crop.
A hundred or sixty or thirty times what was sown.

Ask any gardener—good soil rarely just happens.
Good soil is the result of work—it has had the weeds removed painstakingly
    by hand.
It has been dug, and turned, fed and enriched.
It has been prepared.

This may take several seasons.
Open your heart and allow God to begin.[7]

Do You Want to Be Healed?

[First read the healing story in John 5:1–9.]

You unsettle me, Jesus;
this loving provocation of yours—
What can you do for me?
What have you done for me lately?
Have I told you lately . . .

So why this question?
Why not a question about need?
Ask me what I need Jesus;
I can talk that language;
I can justify that,
Everyone needs, you know that?

Want is confusing,
What you want . . .
Tell me what you want, what you really, really . . .
But you can't always get it.

If I tell you, you will have me in a corner,
I will be too vulnerable,
I might not want it after all,
I might not want to live up to my wants,
I might not be brave enough to be a "have."
My wants allow me to be a "have-not";
The timid fellowship of the deprived.

Or if I tell you, it might all come spilling out,
So much wanting, you might not thank me Jesus,
Wants bigger than I can bear to admit,
Wants that expose me, or reduce me,
humiliate me, disgrace me . . .
Wants that break me, break my faith or break my health or
break my heart . . . break my bank . . .

I want to tell you, but I am more afraid
that if I tell,
you will not give me what I want.
Where will I be then?
And what will be the use of this prayer?

And what will it say about you?
And will you have your usual alibis?

Would I rather wait like the poet
for "the angel's rare, random descent."
But she killed herself, didn't she?

What are you saying?
How do I read this?
Is my faith paralyzed?

Is this a trick question?

Do you want to heal me?[8]

Jesus Give Us Courage

[Two voices, one leading the response.]

Jesus you fasted alone for 40 days
you pushed yourself to the limits
you faced your demons and met your angels
We ask you to be in our fasting
Jesus give us courage
Jesus give us courage

Jesus you feasted with outcasts
you broke down the barriers that divided people
by sharing food and drink
We ask you to be in our feasting

Jesus give us courage
Jesus give us courage

Jesus you had a passion for a life of extremes
you taught us that to live we have to be prepared to die
to eat we have to be prepared to fast
to love others we have to learn to be alone
We ask you to be in our living
Jesus give us courage
Jesus give us courage

Jesus may we live your life with you and share in your death.
May we have the courage to walk with you,
to stare death in the face and to love life. Amen.[9]

Lent Identity

Who are you when your job and place in society are taken away—what's left
   that can't be taken away? What is the irreducible hardcore you?
What is the you of you?
Is all we have the identities that society has given us—our style, our clothing
   labels, our jobs, our cars, our political choices? Are these like clothes that
   we pull around our naked selves? Will we shiver and catch cold without
   them, or be arrested for indecent exposure of the soul?

So who are you going to be today? We're lost in a world full of choices. In
   the past, who you were was given to you by birth and occupation, and
   few escaped their place. Now "who am I?" is a decision we have to make
   for ourselves every day, and a lot of the time we don't know where to
   begin . . .

So we drift through identities, always acting, reinventing ourselves on the
   outside but never able to change ourselves on the inside; or we live and
   die by who other people say we are. We don't know how to define ourselves except by the categories that our society offers us, so we shoehorn
   ourselves in, grateful for the security of a label, grateful to belong, even if
   we have to cut off bits of our inner selves to fit in the box . . .

A lot of us are told we're worthless, and that becomes our identity, tainting
   everything we do with the stench of failure, making even our virtues or
   successes seem provisional and temporary in the face of our fundamental
   loserdom.

Those that have success find that it isn't enough to fill a heart, unless you
   shrink it . . .

And when the rest of us find that we don't have the talent for the premier division, or the head office, or the A-levels, we know that we are failures, because success is the only success, and we live out our lives knowing that we were not good enough . . .

At the beginning of his public ministry, after he had been baptized by John the Baptist, Jesus went into the desert to find out who he was if he wasn't going to be a carpenter any more. Interestingly Luke, in his gospel, puts in Jesus' genealogy, his family tree, at this point—this is how Jesus' fellow Jews defined who he was—later, when Jesus starts preaching in the synagogue in Nazareth, his fellow Nazarenes are outraged at his presumption—who does he think he is, they say, isn't he just Joseph's son? In their society, where family defines who you are, they think they know all about him by knowing his family.

So Jesus goes out into the desert, away from the pigeonholes of job and family, to ask God who he really is. And by the end of the 40 days, Satan's repeated question "if you are the son of God . . ." tells us that Jesus had found out.

So who does God think you are?

In the desert all the things that we use to define our identities are missing, and we are left with nothing except what we have inside. A lot of us fear that we would find we had nothing inside, or only fear and pain, and so we never venture into the desert. In the desert there is nowhere to hide, if God comes to us, as he came to Jesus, as he came to Moses, as he came to Jacob, to show us who we really are to him. And we clutch our thin rags of identity to us like armor, and shrink back from his touch—better the little we have, we say, than risk even that being taken away as well.

But those who try to save their life will lose it all, and God needs to strip us naked, in spite of our fear and embarrassment—and if we let him remove these filthy rags, and wash the wounds, he will reclothe us as something we never imagined, or only caught glimpses of in dreams and ran after down the High Street, but found that the things we bought could never quite get us there, because we were still wearing the same old stinking underwear underneath—and when we put on the identity God offers us—the one he sewed himself, until his hands bled—we will know that we have become our real selves at last, we have found out who we really are, that we are free, and need never search, lost, through the world again . . .

And maybe the desert turns out to be a beach, after all, so we make a bonfire of those old rags and watch the sun rise over the ocean . . .[10]

Noise

noise is unwanted sound
which is why your parents call the music you like noise

but noise isn't just about sound
it's about information
noise is whatever drowns out or interferes with or conceals
meaningful information
sound engineers, radio engineers speak of two things, signal and noise
the signal is the message, the meaningful part of the transmission
the noise is all the unwanted stuff that interferes with your
ability to hear or decipher the signal
our lives are full of noise
too much information
too many messages that don't add up to any coherent whole
all competing for our attention we can't find the signal or make
any sense of our lives

and so we go into the desert to escape the noise

but then we can hear our internal noise
some of which is very gross especially during silent prayer
and some of which is subtle but more deeply disturbing
like tinnitus which is nerve damage to the inner ear resulting in a
permanent whistling or hissing noise inside your head that
you can never escape

and that's just the physical noise inside us
but our heads are full of mental noise
the thoughts that won't stop chattering that stupid song that
you can't get out of your head that nagging worry about
something you said or didn't say
that hurt and anger that you can't let go of, churning inside you
when you're supposed to be concentrating on work that dumb
joke that keeps making you giggle on the bus so that people
look at you strangely . . .
and when you're alone you can't pretend any more that any of
these were necessary
so you try and put them aside to pray

and now you become aware of spiritual noise

all those things that compete with God
distracting your attention towards selfish or worldly concerns

drowning out your attempts to hear God's voice distorting the message
or making you lose bits like a mobile phone passing under a bridge

sin is a kind of spiritual tinnitus
the closer we get to God's silence the more we are aware of
the unceasing whine inside ourselves
of want and need and hurt and self
trouble is we've lost the volume knob and anyway we're
scared of silence because without all the activity and
distractions
we'll have to face ourselves and God and we are frightened of
what we might find
but God longs to heal us
to still the oscilloscopes of our souls
turn the noise off
and give us peace
because only then
will we be able to hear
the music of heaven[11]

Reading the Bible

How do you read the Bible?
Do you read the Bible?
Why do you read the Bible?

How often do you read it?
Do you read little and often, or great chunks occasionally?
Have you read it cover-to-cover?
Have you ever read more than a single chapter at one go?
Have you ever read it aloud?

Where do you read it?
On the train where everyone can see?
Or at home where no-one can see?

Which version do you prefer?
Do you go for word-for-word translation of the Hebrew and Greek or
an easy-to-read paraphrase?

Is the Bible too heavy?
Would you like it to be broken up into its individual books so you didn't
have to take all of them to your small group?
If it was broken up, would you put some books on one side and never
read them?

If you had to buy the books separately, would you buy the whole set or
only some?
If only some, which, and why?

Which books of the Bible have you never read from?
   Why?
Which bits are your favorites?
   Why?

Do you struggle to relate it to your own life?
Or does it speak directly to you?

Do you take every word as inspired?
Do you take every word as true?
Do you think it contains mistakes?

What bugs you about the Bible?
Genocide? Sexism? Patriarchy? Ritualized animal murder?
Which bits frighten you?
Which bits reassure you?

How do you read the Bible? Do you read the Bible?
Why do you read the Bible?[12]

Promised Land

[This liturgy/ritual was inspired by Martin Luther King's famous speech "I've
been to the mountaintop," 1968. His oratory is inspirational. If you can get a
recording of the speech (via the internet or on CD) it works well to mix the
speech in with some music — something instrumental and upbeat is ideal.]

I don't know what will happen now. We've got some difficult days ahead. But
it doesn't matter with me now because I've been to the mountaintop. And I
don't mind. Like anybody I would like to live a long life; longevity has its place.
But I'm not concerned about that now. I just want to do God's will. And he's
allowed me to go up to the mountain. And I've looked over. And I've seen the
promised land. I may not get there but I want you to know tonight that we as a
people will get to the promised land. And I'm happy tonight, I'm not worried
about anything. I'm not fearing any man. Mine eyes have seen the coming of
the glory of the Lord. (MLK)

[Invite people to write their dream of a promised land down on a sheet of
paper. People then read them out. At the end they say "I may not get there"
to which everyone replies "we as a people will get to the promised land."]

Confession

[Each person takes the dream of the person next to them.]

Our dreams of the promised land are in one another's hands

I have a dream tonight
I have a dream of a faster car
I have a dream of a bigger house
I have a dream of a beautiful lover

You may not get there with me but I want you to know that I as an
individual will get to the promised land

I have a dream of profitable investments
I have a dream of celebrity
I have a dream of another beautiful lover

You may not get there with me but I want you to know that I as an
individual will get to the promised land

I have a dream of political influence
I have a dream of new markets
I have a dream of a level playing field

You may not get there with me but I want you to know that I as an
individual will get to the promised land

One more won't make any difference
Why should my standard of living suffer
I can do what I like with my own money

You may not get there with me but I want you to know that I as an
individual will get to the promised land

This land belongs to my ancestors
They come here and take our jobs
This development will bring benefits to everyone

You may not get there with me but I want you to know that I as an
individual will get to the promised land

[tear dreams in half]

Our dreams of the promised land are in one another's hands

We have trampled one another's dreams in the race to seize our own
We have built our promised lands on the ruins of other people's homes
We have pursued short term paradise at the cost of an ancient beauty

Jesus said "you shut the kingdom of heaven in people's faces. You do not
enter yourselves nor will you let those enter who are trying to"

In the pursuit of our own promised lands we deny others the greatest
promised land of all—that of your kingdom

We shut the door of your kingdom in other people's faces when we
construct our own empires
We rob them of the knowledge of its existence when we fail to embody
it in our lives
We condemn others to promised lands that can't deliver and don't
endure
We conceal or forget the promised land that gives wholeness forever

Have pity on us for we have torn one another
And in tearing one another we tore you
But your tearing is our mending
We give up our self centered visions
And ask you to bind us into your mysterious dream. The promised land
whose pattern we have barely caught. Amen[13]

Big Confession

In this prayer we are using fast food as a cultural symbol of our time, but we
all share in the values and principles that fast food represents. We eat the food
we make. For legal reasons, we cannot produce this piece exactly as it was
used. You may want to relate "Big Confession" to a specific chain of fast-food
outlets in your locality.

Hungry God—Have mercy on us.

Christ of the wilderness hear our confession:

We are what we eat, we confess our sin,
this is our temple, where we have our fast feasts.
We are ready to enjoy a happy meal, but not to eat a meal of
sadness for injustice.
Hungry God—Have mercy on us.

We are ready to be scared about Mad Cow Disease for our own children, but
not to fear the effects of starvation for the children of others.

Hungry God—Have mercy on us.

We are ready to throw away our containers and to throw away
our rainforests.
We are ready to eat Big Burgers in any city in the world, but not
to mourn the death of cultures.
Hungry God—Have mercy on us.

We are ready to enjoy the cheapness of the prices, but not to
grumble for the low wages of those who work there.
We are ready to think that Big Burger is better Burger, but not to
think that small is beautiful.
Hungry God—Have mercy on us.

We are ready to send our fathers there on Saturdays, but not to
demand they are there for their children the rest of the week.
We are ready to see the brightness of the colors but not
the loneliness on the faces.
Hungry God—Have mercy on us.

We are ready for the clown and his good causes, but not to change the world
    ourselves.
Hungry God—Have mercy on us.

We are ready to eat fast food, but not to make slow relationships.
Hungry God—Have mercy on us.

We are ready to eat fast food, but not to fast.
Hungry God—Have mercy on us.[14]

We Are Hungry

Look at us, Lord
Our hands are empty
Our hearts are hungry
What do we want?
We are hungry for you, God our maker

We are hungry for a world where people are loved and affirmed
We are hungry for you, Holy Spirit
We are hungry for justice
We are hungry for community
We are hungry for celebration
We are hungry for you, Jesus Christ
We are hungry for change[15]

You Are Hungry

God of life,
Today we remember that you are hungry too;
Jesus Christ, your wilderness hunger
Has prepared this feast;
Your hunger for life drove you to make yourself
into food for the life of the world;
In our hearts we celebrate your life and death and life from death,
And we proclaim
This bread will be for us your body,
This wine will be for us your blood

So we do now, what you did at the last feast,
On the night you were betrayed,
Gathered with your friends
Around a table, you took bread and wine;
You said they were your body broken and your blood poured out,
A new relationship to God.[16]

I Believe in Jesus

I believe in Jesus,
who rose from the river
to see heaven opened
to the Spirit falling and the Father calling:
"I love you"

I believe in Jesus,
who walked to the desert
to be tried and tempted
with the Spirit leading and the devil calling:
"If you are"

I believe in Jesus,
who stayed forty days there,
as he prayed and fasted
with his guts hurting and his breath smelling
"Turn these stones"

I believe in Jesus,
who went with the devil
to be offered power
with the wild beasts roaring and the angels chanting
"Worship God"

I believe in Jesus,
who looked down on the city,
with a fear of falling
with the angels watching and the hard earth waiting
"It is written"

I believe in Jesus,
truly God, truly human,
who was sorely tempted,
with the same temptations we all are facing
"Yet without sin"[17]

Closing Blessing — Losing My Religion

Now go in peace,
leave behind childish things
lose the religion imposed on you by others
in all of your choices choose truth freely

but look for the hope of a new childhood
and search for the kingdom of God
and find that truth and God are not enemies

The presence of Jesus Christ,
the Way, the Truth and the Life
Go with us all, Amen[18]

End Prayer

Lord God, guardian of the wild spaces,
of feasts on mountaintops and mugs of coffee in snow,
of cagouled cloudy beaches and headlights at midnight on the motorway,
thank you that we find in the bread and the wine a space to be with you.
Throw us the compass of who we are and whose we are;
let your hope be a big sky within us;
let your presence be sand in our pockets.[19]

Rituals

DISTRACTIONS

DISTRACTIONS

Items needed

A compass, set of 3 or 4 magnets, a large map.

Instructions for setting up

Spread the map out on the floor. Place the compass in the middle and the magnets around the edges of the map.

Description

Invite people to move the magnets near to the compass and see how they pull the needle away from north. Then encourage them to reflect on what distractions/false norths are pulling their focus away from God/true north.

The "distractions" meditation below was written to accompany this ritual and could be read aloud or printed and laminated and placed by the map.

Distractions Meditation

In front of you is a map
In the center is a compass
The needle of the compass points directly north
Also on the map are some small magnets, some "false norths"

Try moving these magnets around the compass
See what happens
The "false norths" pull the needle away from true north

If God is true north what are the false norths distracting your
focus away from God?
As you identify these false norths move them to the edge of
the map

Refocus on true north . . .

Begin to focus on God

Other ideas

The distractions meditation could work as a stand alone meditation without
setting up the station.[20]

CONTEMPORARY DESERT

Items needed

Car seats (some cars have seats that are removable — if you can't get access to
one of those use some other suitable seats), several CD Discmans, a selection
of CDs with music that enables you to have a sense of space (some ambient
instrumental music would be ideal or something with a lyric that evokes
something of God), a video filmed out of a car front window driving through
or stuck in traffic in your town, a VCR and ideally a video projector.

Instructions for setting up

The idea is to set up a station that simulates a car journey. Project the video
of traffic on to a large screen. Set up the car seats facing the screen. Place
a Discman with headphones on each seat either with a CD in or with the
selection of CDs in a rack so that people can choose one to listen to.

Description

For a lot of people, traveling in their car with the stereo on is the closest
they get to solitude. Setting up this ritual will hopefully help people to reflect
positively on the space they have next time they are driving alone in the car. So
the ritual is simply sitting and having some space listening to music to reflect

and pray. For most of us going to an actual desert is not a realistic option. We need to find ways to find a bit of space and desert in the midst of our otherwise busy lives. Perhaps the car journey is a contemporary equivalent of desert.

Other ideas

This can work without the video projection — just set up the car seats and Discmans.

We haven't gone this far but how about getting an actual (small) car in the worship space and using that?![21]

Finding Identity in the Desert

Items needed

A tray of sand; enough pieces of paper with the "promises in the sand" or equivalent written or typed out on them.

Instructions for setting up

Print out pieces of paper with promises of what God says about identity. You could use the piece "Promises in the Sand" below or make up your own. Make sure that there are enough for everyone to have one. Roll the pieces of paper up like small scrolls and place them in a tray of sand.

Description

This ritual accompanies the idea of retreating into the desert away from the noise of everyday life. When all is stripped away and there's nothing left but you and God what might God say about who you are? To symbolize finding identity in the desert invite people to come and take one of the scrolls from the tray of sand. Then leave plenty of space for them to meditate and chew over the promises. It would be good to play some suitable background music. This would be a very good ritual to follow on from the reading "Lent Identity" (pages 75–76).

Promises in the Sand

You are fearfully and wonderfully made.
I molded you in the depths of the earth and knit you together in your mother's womb.
I chose you before the foundation of the world.
You are my child, made in my image.
I have called you by name, you are mine.

As a father has compassion for his child I have compassion for you and I love
    you as much as a mother intimately loves her child.
I know the number of the hairs on your head, the details of your life,
your smile your tears, your hopes and fears. You are precious to me.
Your name is written in the palm of my hand. I will never forget you.
My love for you isn't based on what you have done or will do for me.
I love you for who you are—the you of you.
You don't have to strive or perform for my approval.
My favor rests on you.
You are beloved.
I will never leave you or forsake you.
I will always be with you.
You are mine.
Rest in my love.

Other ideas

You could write out individual promises or verses rather than use the
"Promises in the Sand" piece.

A desert service like this is greatly enhanced by having images evocative
of a desert.

You could cover the whole worship space with sand so that the whole
worship experience conveys the desert. (It may take a while to clear up
though!)[22]

IMPRESSION

Items needed

A sandbox, sand, a towel.

Instructions for setting up

Set up the sandbox with the sand in it smoothed over and a towel next
to it.

Description

Invite people to take off their socks and shoes and to stand in the sand to
make an impression. After they have done so they should step back and reflect
on what impression they have and are leaving with their life. The meditation
"Impression" (see pages 71–72) could be printed and laminated and placed
by the sandbox or read out loud as an accompanying meditation.

Other ideas

Instead of the impression meditation you could use the footprints as a way of encouraging people to reflect on their life's journey in the last few months.

A video loop of feet walking on the beach or desert makes a great backdrop.[23]

IMPOSITION OF ASHES

Items needed

Ash.

Instructions for setting up

You need to make some ash. Traditionally this is made by burning the previous year's palm crosses which are then mixed with a bit of oil. This makes a kind of paste that means that the ash leaves a mark on the forehead.

Description

The imposition of ashes is a traditional ritual that takes place on Ash Wednesday at the start of Lent. It is a very sobering ritual. While it has been maintained in many parts of the church, in others it has been almost completely ignored. Each worshiper is invited to come forward to receive the imposition of ashes. They are marked on the forehead with ash by the priest who says these or similar words: "Remember that you are dust and to dust you shall return. Turn from your sin and be faithful to Christ."

To be reminded of our own humanity and frailty and to be called to repentance is a powerful thing.

Other ideas

Rather than one or two persons making the mark on people's foreheads it is possible to do the ritual such that one person marks the first person and says the appropriate words. They then take the ash and mark the next and so on. This could either be done by passing the ash around or by forming a line.[24]

PRAYERS IN SAND

Items needed

Sandbox, sand, towel.

Instructions for setting up

Set up the sandbox with the sand in it smoothed over.

Description

Invite people to write prayers in the sand or make prayers in the sand. This could tie in with a Lent service on the desert. Or it can work well for a confession where once people have written their confession they can smooth the sand over and see that what they have confessed has gone.[25]

SAND AND WATER

Items needed

A tray of sand, bottles or cups of water.

Instructions for setting up

Have a space set up with cups or bottles of water and sand. The sand could be in a bowl or on a tray, or if you have used it earlier in the service in a sandbox or as part of a desert service, people could take some of that sand.

Description

For some people Lent is a call to the desert for a season, to solitude, to getting away, to spending time alone with God. Taking some sand and putting it in your pocket is a way of acknowledging that you need some desert. Every time you put your hand in your pocket in the following week the sand will be there to remind you.

For others the desert is a place of dryness that expresses their own current experience of life and relation to God. They already feel in the desert. Taking some water is a way of acknowledging this dryness and asking God for an oasis, for some refreshment, for some relief from the desert.

So invite people to come forward and either take some sand and place it in their pockets or to take a drink of water, depending on what response they want to make.

Other ideas

The prayer "End Prayer" (page 84) relates well to those taking sand.[26]

LETTING GO

Items needed

A large bowl or container two-thirds full of water (a plastic trash can will do), a pile of stones (enough for everyone present to have one each).

Instructions for setting up

Place the stones in a pile next to the bowl or container of water.

Description

The ritual is very simple—take a stone, imagine the pressures, cares, and worries you are carrying. Drop the stone in the water as a way of letting go of them and offering them to God. The meditation below could either be read out to accompany this or printed out and laminated and placed by the stones for people to read.

Letting Go Meditation

Take some deep slow breaths and relax
Begin to let go of the tensions in your body
Feel the pressure and busyness slipping away
As you draw breath think of how your body is using oxygen—it is being
carried to every part of your body—feel the life it brings
As you exhale, you breathe out carbon dioxide which you don't need
Trees and plants take this in
They then produce oxygen which sustains you
You are an integral part of God's creation

In front of you is a pile of stones and a pool of water
Take a stone from the pile
Imagine all of your concerns and worries are held in the stone
Hold the stone tightly and name the concerns and worries in your mind
In your own time let it go
Watch your concerns and worries fall
Imagine them falling into God's lap
How does it feel to release them?

Other ideas

An outdoor version of this is to stand on the edge of the beach or a lake or a cliff and imagine the pressures, cares, and worries and then throw the stone as far as possible into the sea or lake.[27]

BREATHING

Items needed
None.

Instructions for setting up
Encourage people to sit in a comfortable position.

Description
This way of praying should be led slowly, perhaps with accompanying music that isn't distracting. The idea is simply that as everyone breathes in they are encouraged to use that as a way of praying for God to fill them with good things, his life, his love, himself. And as they breathe out to use that as a way of praying to let go of stress, pressure, and so on. The leader might say something like this:

A good way of praying is to relax your body.
    Concentrate on your breathing.
    Take a deep breath in and hold it for a few seconds.
    Then breathe out.
    As you breathe out imagine breathing out everything that you want to let go of. Then as you breathe in ask God to fill you with his love and presence.

Breathe in love	Breathe out hate
Breathe in life	Breathe out death
Breathe in peace	Breathe out anxiety
Breathe in gentleness	Breathe out tension

Breathe in God's presence

Breathe out all that distracts us from God[28]

HANDS

Items needed
None

Instructions for setting up
Encourage people to sit in a comfortable position and to close their eyes.

Description

This is a way of praying where people clench their hands tight to picture the things they are holding on to. Then slowly open them as a way of offering those things to God. They then turn them upwards as a way of asking God to fill them with his Spirit. The leader might say something like this:

Close your eyes and clench your hands up tight.

Imagine all the pressures and worries and tensions you are carrying as you come to worship.

Then in your own time gently turn your hands over so that they are facing down. Imagine God's hands underneath yours and slowly open your hands so that the things you are carrying fall into God's hands.

You may wish to repeat this several times.

Then turn your hands face up, but this time with the palms open and ask God's Spirit to fill you afresh.

Other ideas

Visual images of hands open and closed are very powerful. They make a good backdrop.[29]

Images

The church has been arguing for centuries about images in worship. The arguments were rooted in how to understand the Old Testament prohibitions on idolatry. Many of the Reformers reacted against the extravagant aesthetics of medieval Catholicism by stripping the worship space and turning it back into a minimal functional auditorium.

Alt worship has turned back towards imagery, but has embraced it in new ways. This may be the most distinctive and powerful innovation within the worship of emerging churches, and it remains a focus for debate and critical engagement. When Sheffield's Nine O'Clock Service first appeared, the most striking thing about its services was how they looked. Young people trained in late twentieth-century visual arts and media had taken over the worship environment and remodeled it in striking and unexpected ways. Other alt worship groups have tackled this in distinctive ways, driven by different artistic visions, but everywhere there has been a great deal of playfulness and experimentation. People have asked new questions: "What would it feel like to say or sing this, while watching this?" "What would it feel like to start with this image and bring words or music to it?"

Previously, people had used tape—slide sequences in evangelistic settings and sometimes for meditative moments in church services, but this was on a different scale. Photography was an art form untried and uncritiqued in the worship of the church. Now you could take Uncle John's old slide projector (sew a few white sheets together if the walls weren't bare enough), turn the lights out, and enact the most astonishing visual transformation of the least promising of spaces. Marry this with the calls from people like Walter Brueggemann for a new prophetic imagination and alt worshipers found themselves in a place of remarkable cultural relevance and challenge.

94

Images are used by alt worshipers in a whole range of ways. Some are very simple, others are in the forefront of contemporary artistic expression.

- Images of ordinary things, of your everyday surroundings, can have enormous meaning used in church, perhaps with a meditation or prayer. They can be a way of bringing your familiar environment before God and of seeing it in new ways, perhaps through God's eyes.
- Slides and video images can be used at different paces. If you change them often or use fast-moving video, people will tend to watch them like TV in case they miss something. Be sure you want this before you do it.
- Multiple screens and multiple speeds can prevent the focus being taken by one frontal location.
- Don't be pressurized into feeling you need elaborate and extended visual sequences all the time. It may be better to have three well-chosen static images that will be memorable and meaningful for people. Sometimes the images will be background, sometimes they will be foreground.
- Every group will have some people who have a more natural feel for using images. Often their gifts will not have been valued or used by churches in the past. Photographers and artists have been pew fodder, while wordsmiths and musicians dictated the content of worship. Get an art student to sit down with a sales executive and devise a new kind of PowerPoint presentation—both will have skills to bring to the project.
- Slides can look fantastic when projected around the worship space. Borrow projectors—as many as possible. Even old clapped out ones may carry static images fine. Take your own photographs. Get some people taking slides on a theme. Use shots of creation, elemental stuff (e.g. water, fire), stained-glass windows, icons, abstracts, bread and wine. Purchase slides. Cathedrals and art galleries often have collections. With several projectors you can project images at various places in the room. Use sheets, muslin, or a parachute. You can project onto walls or the ceiling. If you use muslin, there'll be a better effect if the surface isn't too smooth. Try creating some depth and layers. Try projecting from behind. Your imagination is the limit.
- Have someone or several people engage with the theme of a service by making a painting during the worship. This might be best done by people who have some experience as artists and who may choose to prepare the picture beforehand.

- Have paints/paper/clay available for people to draw/paint/model during the worship, then take photos of what has been produced and use it another time on slide. Hang the pictures around the place. People will need encouraging to try this kind of thing. Also the process of expressing something is as important as the end product.
- Encourage others to produce stuff in advance either to have as sculpture or paintings, or to photograph and use on slide.

Liturgy

One of the things alt worship groups have rediscovered is the notion of liturgy as "the work of the people."[30] The origins of the word "liturgy" are related to this idea. (Sadly the l-word now makes most people think of officially sanctioned words and prayers, owned, produced, and controlled by "experts" and institutions.)

In an alt worship community the process of planning a worship service usually involves a number of shared planning sessions. Having agreed on a theme, one meeting might be a brainstorming of ideas. Some of these will then be picked up and developed at further meetings. The resources of the group, their reading of the Bible, 2000 years of tradition, creativity, and contemporary culture are all brought into the mix. There are no recognized experts or professionals directing the process. It helps if a group has some people who have knowledge/theological capital, who know something of the resources and treasures to be found in the tradition, but it helps more if they don't offer them as "the expert." Theirs is just one of the many gifts brought to the group. Other people will bring different skills and talents. Ideas that are developed are then taken on by various group members. One might agree to take some slides, another to make a computer animation, another to write or locate some responsive prayers. Eventually everything on the service plan, from who is doing what, to how the worship space will be laid out, will have been agreed. The liturgy at the worship service is then genuinely the work of the people. Some things will be brilliantly crafted, others a bit hastily flung together, but there is always a sense of excitement in seeing what has been worked on by the people finally become a shared, public liturgy.

Initially this process can be very labor-intensive, but over time groups build up a stock of their best pieces. Not everyone in the community will be involved in this planning process, but the more widely shared it is the more we might say it deserves to be called liturgy!

Music

God likes reggae, techno, and jazz. Dare to believe it. And dare to think again about what music is for in worship and who it's for. Music in worship can be complex, exquisite, raw, experimental, aggressive, delicate, mournful, ecstatic.

Music is to listen to. To walk in or out to. To sing with. It's for young children, or for everybody. To meditate to. To dance to.

You know which music means most to you, speaks to you of God, or of life, so use your own musical culture in worship. Use the soundtrack of your own lives. Challenge the categorization into sacred and secular—often there's no obvious divide.

> At Grace we use "secular" stuff, and people think it's "Christian" because the church context changes the perceived meaning. This can be revelatory, and in turn can stunningly transform the way that the same music is heard in its usual secular context. Keep an ear out for where God is in the "secular" world, where real spiritual issues are being dealt with. There are some surprises to be had.[31]

People who come to church carrying negative emotions or problems can feel alienated or excluded by a constant diet of upbeat joyful worship music. They also need music and words that enable them to articulate their pain to God. A pastoral sense in worship recognizes that this pain may not be healed until it has been given room for expression.

Here are a few suggestions for ways to use music:

- Use music as background or to create atmosphere. Think in terms of a continuous film soundtrack, rather than individual songs. These can be dropped into the general musical flow. The background music provides emotional color, fills gaps, papers over the buzz of conversation in group discussions, etc.
- Do readings, prayers, and spoken stuff over music (often quiet background music is appropriate but not always—mix it up).
- Play tracks with lyrics to listen to and pick out some of the words and project them while the song is playing.
- Stay able to turn it all off and embrace silence.

Part 3

Easter

Resources

hrist is Risen! Alleluia—Christ is Risen! Increasingly ignored and un-noticed as a secular festival, Easter remains the greatest festival of the Christian year. The drama of Holy Week focuses the church's attention ever more closely on the figure of Jesus as he rides into Jerusalem to face arrest, trial, torture, and crucifixion. Maundy Thursday gives an annual authorization in story for the church's communion practice in the present, while rooting it back to the story of Passover and looking forward to the great banquet of the kingdom of heaven.

Good Friday calls the church to "wonder and stare," to contemplate and question what is being done in the cruelty and agony of the Cross. Here the transformation of God begun in Bethlehem is brought to a terrible climax, in the figure of the crucified God, dying outside the human city.

Saturday is, according to the Jewish critic George Steiner, the longest day in western civilization—the day in which Christ waits in the tomb, the day in which the universe waits for resurrection, waits to see if death has won.

Sunday explodes in sound and light, church bells ring, alleluias sing, the colors change from penitence and mourning to extravagant celebration. The sanctuary stripped on Maundy Thursday is lavishly redecked. The fast is swallowed by the feast.

Light, energy, freshly kindled fire, the rising sun—movement, dance, running, celebration, food, festival, holiday—abundant life for all!

Psalm 118
(a free translation into modern English)

Let me in! I've got to get into church;
It's the only place to be when you've dedicated yourself to God.
Thanks for answering my prayers—you saved me!

The stone the builders threw out ended up as the pinnacle.
We thought this was impossible, but God did it!
Our big moment belongs to him, so let's party in his honor.
Lord may you always save us and give us success.

If you've come in God's name, welcome!
Come in and enjoy the good things here.
There's only one God and he's shining his light on us;
Grab a beer and get on the dance floor.

You are my God and I will thank you;
Let me hear you make some noise!
Put your hands in the air for God because he is good;
His love will last for ever.[1]

God on a Stick

They spit on his face and then they crucify him
Jesus our Lord
He dies as a sinner
He dies as a blasphemer, as an idolator, as one who denies God
As one who betrays him

I stand before the cross and wonder
He is not guilty of these things but takes our place

He dies as one who boasts, who gossips
As one who dishonors his parents
As a cheat, as a liar, as a thief
He dies as a fraud and an embezzler

I stand before the cross and fear
He is not guilty of these things but takes our place

He dies as a sinner
he dies as one with evil thoughts
as a slave to lust, as a fornicator
As an adulterer, as an abuser of children

I kneel before the cross and weep
He is not guilty of these things but takes our place

He dies as one full of jealousy
As one who is selfish, unkind and rude
As one who destructively manipulates others

As one who envies and hates
He dies as a sadist
As one who destroys and murders

I pray before the cross and rejoice
He is not guilty of these things but takes our place
He is not to blame but dies to take the blame for us

He is dying to forgive us

Stand, stand . . .
And watch Jesus die
Alone with nothing . . .
God on a stick[2]

The Guest

Jesus himself was a guest at a wedding in Cana
We've heard it all before
He turned water into wine
(It's our proof text against puritans)
Vintage stuff

Jesus was a guest . . . of humanity
The heavenly host who laid on a harvest of abundance for the world
The creator
My provider

Became the guest
Of the animals in the stable
The villagers in Nazareth
The religious leaders in the temple
The prostitutes
Drunkards
Tax collectors

He let us play host,
Did away with the VIP pass
Ate, drank and was probably merry
Became one of us
Dined at our table
Ate the same bread, drank the same wine—
Everybody having a good time
Shared stories
Shared our story

When he left the table
He left bread and wine
He left himself
But left himself
The guest
Once more
Became the consummate Host[3]

Host

When you get invited to a party what do you think?
Does it depend on who's invited you?
The hostess with the mostest?
Or the bachelor with BO?

Does your mind think up an excuse straight away?
Or two, just to be safe?
Or do you clear your calendar and buy a new outfit?
Or two, just to be safe?
If it's BYOB, do you?

Do you become the life and soul?
Or do you simmer quietly in the kitchen?
Do you throw parties?
Or do they throw you?

Do you turn up early?
Turn up late?
Turn up the volume?
Turn it down?
Turn down the invitation?
Turn out to keep up appearances?
Or to keep up with the Joneses?
Or to keep young?
Or to keep moving?
Or just to keep keeping on?

How do you feel if someone turns up uninvited?
(Do you
(a) ask them to leave
(b) welcome them with gritted teeth or
(c) pour them a glass of your best Chablis?)

What if someone you invited doesn't turn up?
(Do you

(a) grin and bear it
(b) phone them to "see if they're all right" or
(c) accidentally forget to send them a Christmas card that year?)

And didn't you go to all that trouble?
Oh it was nothing, I'm sure . . . but you hope they'll take the trouble to notice.
Does it trouble you when they don't?

Do you expect to receive an invite?
Or does that just invite disappointment?
How could you thank someone for being a great host?
Just compliment them?
Or return the compliment?

What does the word "thank" mean?
And how do you say it?
With flowers?
With relish?
With practice?

How do you receive?
Receive attention?
Friendship?
Undeserving love?

Can you hear God's call through the atmospherics and the interference:
"Are you receiving me?
Are you receiving me?
Are you receiving me?"[4]

Let There Be Exodus

[This should be spoken over a slow groove with a sung kyrie at the end.]

Let there be Exodus
Out of the deadly land of our bloody history
Let there be Exodus
Out of the country of poison gas/Out of the country of holocaust
Let there be Exodus
Out of the country of Jew killing /Out of the country of blood spilling
Let there be Exodus
Out of the country of radiation/Out of the country of black starvation
Let there be Exodus
Out of the country of global pollution/Out of the country of bad evolution
Let there be Exodus

Out of the country of white indifference/Out of the country of racist violence
Let there be Exodus
Out of the country of ethnic genocide/Out of the country of global biocide
Let there be Exodus
Out of the country of Communist terror/Out of the country of free market failures
Let there be Exodus
Out of the country of class divisions/Out of the country of weak politicians
Let there be Exodus
Kyrie, have mercy Lord/Kyrie, have mercy Lord

Absolvo/Release

God has made a way,
To all who move out of the old land
God speaks this word

> *In Jesus the lover you are loved*
> *By Jesus the savior you are forgiven*
> *Through Jesus the liberator you are freed*[5]

Jesus in the City

Because you are the Maker and this is your city.
Because your beauty is here for all to see,
We give you thanks:
For the gleam of lights reflected in the river,
For the brightness of rain on a dark street,
For smells of coffee brewing, bacon frying, the baking of tomorrow's bread,
For every sign of your making and sustaining to be found in the city,
We give you thanks and ask you to come close.

Because you are the Savior and this is your city,
Because your love is here for us to touch;
We give you thanks:
For cups of water, chocolate biscuits, parties, needles, chances time, em-
    braces—given in your name;
For masses, eucharists, communions and Lord's Suppers,
A thousand tables graced with broken bread and poured out wine,
The gospel of your love preached and believed in your name, Jesus
    Christ,
For every sign of your saving and liberating presence in the city,
We give you thanks and ask you to come close.

Because you are the Spirit and this is your city,
Because your life is here for us to share,

We worship you, the Lord, the Giver of Life:
For hospitals where women and new-born infants cry for dear life,
For playgrounds where children squeal and shout,
For the laughter of women at work or men at play,
For the sighs of lovers, the prayers of the faithful,
For hospices and homes where hearts will stop and lives will end this night,
For every sign of human life in community, in conflict and in celebration,
And for your comforting, disturbing presence within it,
We give you thanks and ask you to come close.

God of the City,
Maker, Savior, Spirit,
Come close to hear us and speak to us and touch us tonight.
So we pray in Jesus' name, Amen.[6]

Gethsemane

[This meditation is written for two voices and is an exploration of Luke 22:39–46. The first part contains modern parallels, and is unpunctuated to indicate the pace at which it should be read. We used this as part of a service based around Christ's passion, at which several prayer stations could be visited; this meditation comprised one station, and was delivered in its "rolling" format. Two readers are required; they should swap over parts half-way so that each gets to read the Bible passage.]

Jesus went out as usual to the Mount of Olives, and his disciples followed him.

You know what it's like when you're afraid but you can't put your finger on it and you can't relax can't sleep can't rest can't find any place where you feel safe

On reaching the place, he said to them, "Pray that you will not fall into temptation."

Imagine being under threat because of your politics because of your beliefs because of your color because of your creed because of where you've been born

He withdrew about a stone's throw from them . . .

It's hard to face the future when everything ahead seems dark and filled with pain and hate there's no other feeling quite like fear for making you feel isolated and utterly alone

. . . knelt down and prayed.

And if you look at the future look at the news there's fear on everyone's face fear of the future fear of no hope fear of nothing getting better

"Father, if you are willing, take this cup from me."

And everyone's looking for a way out looking for an escape clause looking for a hope for a future for a promise looking for someone who could go there with them instead of them looking for a scapegoat

"Yet not my will but yours be done."

Imagine that what you dread most isn't just a far-off threat or a nightmare but it's real and it's imminent and it's the fear of war of torture of poverty of hunger and the fear is so tangible that you can almost taste it

An angel from heaven appeared to him and strengthened him. And being in anguish, he prayed more earnestly, and his sweat was like drops of blood falling to the ground.

And for so many people around our planet that fear is something they live with every day of their lives something they wake with sleep with breathe in feed on something they can't shake off because it's real and it's happening to them

When he rose from prayer and went back to the disciples, he found them asleep, exhausted from sorrow.

And for the rest of us those of us who live in our stable country in our comfortable homes we too know fear. We worry and fret over our relationships our finances our jobs our families and over the constant changes and shifting sands of our modern culture

"Why are you sleeping?" he asked them.

And you know what it's like to feel betrayed to be let down sold out double-crossed conspired against. You know the pain of being left alone standing in the clearing with the people you thought you could trust the most watching on watching as you're betrayed by the one you love . . .

"Get up and pray so that you will not fall into temptation."

In a garden where a man once faced fear and dread we too are present. We
face the uncertainties of our future or else we sleep, shutting our eyes to
the fears of others.

Jesus went out as usual to the Mount of Olives and his disciples followed him.

Sometimes the hardest paths to walk start with the ordinary and the
mundane.

*On reaching the place he said to them, "Pray that you will not fall into
temptation."*

He knows that we are weak; he knows that we will fail.

He withdrew about a stone's throw from them . . .

He faced what was to come alone, with only God to hear his cry.

. . . knelt down and prayed.

He knelt alone, broken and humble before God.

"Father, if you are willing, take this cup from me."

There was real fear of the unknown, fear of what God wanted him to be.

"Yet not my will but yours be done."

He accepted, placing his body into God's hands
As he would soon place his spirit.

An angel from heaven appeared to him and strengthened him.

God met him—because he was willing
God provided strength—but not a way out

*And being in anguish he prayed more earnestly, and his sweat was like drops of
blood falling to the ground.*

Right through his body he felt the fear,
Right through his body he felt the pain,
Right through his body he felt what was to come.

When he rose from prayer and went back to the disciples he found them asleep,
exhausted from sorrow.

Surrounded by the faithless, he was deserted.

"Why are you sleeping?" he asked them. "Get up and pray so that you will not
fall into temptation."

And it is hard to stand with those in pain
Because of our own fear.
We fail to stand firm,
We fail to take the cup,
And yet
We want to be willing.

[Return to beginning for "rolling" format.][7]

John 21 Meditation

Make yourselves comfortable—
find a position in which you can relax and be still
and when you have found that position
close your eyes.

Now take a deep breath—long, deep, fill your lungs.
Hold it for a few seconds then breathe out—all the way out.

And again a deep breath in—hold—then out again.

Now become aware of the space around you.
Let the walls fade away
leaving you exposed to the night sky and the cold . . .

Several weeks ago, your world fell apart.
When the big test came, you just couldn't cope.
You blew it for yourself
and you blew it for someone else when they needed you more than ever.

And so you left the city and came back to a place where they wouldn't
know what you'd done
and took up the job you'd left in the days of hope.

And now it is after midnight
and you are alone
in a boat on a lake.

The net is over the side, submerged in the water
and you are waiting.

Draw up the net.
How do you feel when the net comes up empty?

Let the net down again.
Watch it slip away silently into the water

and wait. Watch the water. Watch the sky. And listen.

Then draw up the net again.
It is still empty.
How do you feel?
Let it down again into the water, maybe in a different place.

And wait. Watch and listen.
Are you sleepy or alert?

Draw up the net.
How do you feel when it comes up empty the third time?

Row the boat to a different place.
Let the net down again.
Are you hopeful? Are you resigned? Frustrated?

Wait.

Draw up the net.
It is empty.
How do you react?

You have come back to something you know well how to do,
and now even that skill has deserted you.
How does it feel to be a failure?

It is beginning to get lighter.
The sky is turning from black to blue.
It is cold.
There is a mist drifting in patches on the lake.
Above it you see the hills silhouetted against the slowly brightening sky.

Far off on the shore, you hear a bird start to sing.

What kind of song is it?
Is it melodious or harsh?
Few notes or many?

At first it is alone.
Then another starts to sing, a different song;
then two more, then many at once and you cannot count them any more.
Listen to the dawn chorus.
There is no other sound except the gentle waves against the boat.

Something moves on the shore.
You cannot make it out clearly through the drifting mist.
There it is again.

What is it?
An animal? Or a person?

It is a person.
How do you feel?
Are you glad to see them or not?
Do you want to meet them?

Suddenly the person on the shore is calling to you
asking you if you have caught anything.
Will you lie to them or admit your failure?

Now they are telling you where to let down your nets.
How do you feel? You are the fisherman. Who are they?
Are you going to take their advice?

Row the boat to a different place.
Let the net down again.
Are you hopeful? Are you resigned? Frustrated?

Wait.

Draw up the net.
It is full
How do you react?

The net is too full to drag into the boat, so you start to row
towards the shore, hoping it won't break.

Suddenly the first light of the rising sun breaks over the hills
and across the shore, full onto the stranger.
And you see who it is.

It is Jesus.
The friend you have hurt.
How do you feel?
Are you glad to see him or not?
Do you want to meet him?

As you approach the shore you see that Jesus has already lit a fire.
There is a smell of cooking fish
but you don't understand where he got them.

As you step out of the boat he comes to meet you.
Your eyes meet.

What do you see there?
How do you feel?
What are you going to say?
He seems not to notice your feelings.
He offers you breakfast.
You eat in silence.

After breakfast, you and Jesus walk along the shore.
He asks you if you are really his friend.
How do you feel? What is your reply?
He asks you if you are really his friend again.
How do you feel at being asked twice? What is your reply?
He asks you if you even like him.
How do you feel now? How do you reply?

He has something he wants you to do for him.
How do you feel?
How do you feel when he tells you this is something only you can do?
When he tells you that this time you won't fail?

What is it that he is inviting you to do?
That only you can do?
Ask him about it.
Be open about your fears and questions.
What are his answers?
Are you going to accept?

When you have decided
say goodbye for now to Jesus
and get back into the boat.

Put out into the lake
in the blazing sunshine of a new day.

The sun is warm
and your eyes are closed.

Slowly become aware of this space again.
As you do so
bring with you
any insights you have had
into the world after worship.

Now open your eyes.[8]

Eucharist — Hospitality

RITUAL OF WELCOME

[When people arrive for the worship make them welcome. Have some people at the door to shake their hands, take their coats, and perhaps offer them a cup of tea or other appropriate drink.]

WELCOME AND OPENING SENTENCES

Welcome to the communion service. The service follows a simple liturgy around the theme of hospitality.

God the Creator is a gracious, abundant and generous host
You are invited to be guests at God's table
Make yourself at home
Relax
God is here
You are welcome

Listen to the words of Jesus:
"Who needs a doctor: the healthy or the sick? . . . I'm here to invite outsiders, not coddle insiders."
"The wretched of the earth learn that God is on their side."
"Are you tired? Worn out? Burned out on religion? Come to me"
(Matthew 9:12–13; 11:5, 28)

And the words of Paul:
"You're no longer strangers or outsiders. You belong here . . ."
(Ephesians 2)

OPENING PRAYER

Gracious God
You have shared with us the gift of Creation
Open our hearts to receive you here

Jesus Friend of Sinners
You have shared with us the gift of your Incarnation
Open our hearts to receive you here

Spirit of God
You have shared with us the gift of life
Open our hearts to receive you here

PRAISE

CONFESSION

For the times when we have rejected your generous hospitality
Forgive us Lord
For the times when we were too busy or too lazy to come to your party
Forgive us Lord
For the times when we constructed lame excuses
Forgive us Lord

For our failure to extend the gift of hospitality to others
Forgive us Lord
For the times when we have restricted hospitality to those who are
powerful, influential or wealthy
Forgive us Lord
For the times when we have excluded the sad, poor and marginalized
Forgive us Lord

Lord God we remember those who have been excluded by us as
individuals and by the church we represent.
In rejecting them we have rejected you.
For the times we have misrepresented you Lord with our individual and
collective inhospitality
Please forgive us Lord

READINGS

[Read a suitable passage from the Scriptures on the theme of hospitality. The meditations "The Guest" (pages 105–106) and "Host" (pages 106–107) could also be used.]

THE EUCHARIST

Prayer of thanksgiving

Creator God, thank you that you are a gracious, abundant and generous host. But thank you that you became the guest of humanity. The heavenly host, the creator, became the guest of the animals in the stable, the villagers of Nazareth, the religious leaders in the temple, the prostitutes, drunkards, tax collectors. You let us play host, became one of us, dined at our table. You ate the same bread, drank the same wine — everybody having a good time. You shared stories, shared our story. When you left the table, you left bread and wine to remember you by . . .

Holy holy holy Lord
God of power and might
Heaven and earth are full of your glory
Hosanna in the highest

Your death on the cross has enabled us to be guests at God's table. Grant that by the power of the Holy Spirit these gifts of bread and wine may be for us his body and blood who on the night he was betrayed took bread, gave you thanks, broke it and gave it to his disciples saying "take eat, this is my body which is given for you." After supper he took the cup, gave you thanks, and said to them: "this is my blood of the new covenant which is shed for you and for many for the forgiveness of sins. Do this in remembrance of me."

Christ has died
Christ has risen
Christ will come again

Invitation

The table of Jesus is your place of gathering
Here you are welcomed, wanted, loved
Here there is a place set for you

So come all you who thirst
All you who hunger for the bread of life
All you whose souls cry out for healing

Come all you who are weary
All you who are bowed down with worry
All you who ache with the tiredness of living

Come all you poor
All you who are without food or refuge
All you who go hungry in a fat land

Come all you who are lost
All you who search for meaning but cannot find it
All you who have no place of belonging

Jesus invites you
Draw near with faith
Receive the body of our Lord Jesus Christ which he gave for you and his
    blood which he shed for you
Eat and drink in remembrance that Christ died for you and feed on him in
    your hearts by faith with thanksgiving

Share Bread and Wine

Prayer

Ritual of Parting

[Have a visitor's book and invite people to write their comments or a prayer
to God the Host before they leave.]

Blessing

The blessing of God, Host of creation,
The blessing of Christ, Guest of humanity
The blessing of the Holy Spirit, Source of communion
Be with you all.
As you have received the gift of hospitality, go now
Share your life, your table and your home with others in God's name,
Amen.[9]

We Believe in Life

We believe in the God of Life
The world maker, the starlighter,
The sun shiner, the beauty maker;
Provoking evolution from nothing but words of love.
We believe in life.

We believe in the risen Jesus,
The cross bearer, the tomb raider,
The hell-harrower, the death defier;
Embracing resurrection as the first-born from death.
We believe in life.

We believe in the Easter Spirit,
The life-giver, the breath bringer,
The body lover, the church birther,
Enabling communion with Jesus the Living One.
We believe in life.

We believe in the God of Life,
World-maker, cross bearer, life-giver
Trinity of hope leading creation to its liberation.
We believe in God.[10]

The New Glasgow

I saw a vision—it was last Thursday at eleven o'clock in the morning:

I was standing on the Necropolis, looking down over the city;
and the cold blue winter sky broke open above my head
and the Spirit of God breathed on my eyes
and my eyes were opened.

I saw Glasgow, the holy city, coming down out of heaven;
shining like a rare jewel, sparkling like "clear water in the eye of the sun";
and all the sickness was gone from the city,
there were no more suburbs and schemes;
no difference between Bearsden and Drumchapel.

I saw the Clyde running with the water of life,
as bright as crystal,
as clear as glass,
    the children of Glasgow swimming in it.

And the Spirit showed me the tree of life
growing on Glasgow Green.

I looked out and there were no more homeless people,
no more women working the streets,
no more needles in the alleys,
HIV and AIDS were things of the past,
there were no more racist attacks,
no more gay bashing,

no more rapists,
no more stabbings,
no more Protestants and Catholics,
no more IRA graffiti, no more Orange marches,
because there was no more hate!

And I saw women walking safe at nights,
saw the men were full of passion and gentleness,
that none of the children were ever abused,
because the people's sex was full of justice and of joy.

I saw an old woman throw back her head
and laugh like a young girl;
and when the sky closed back, her laughter rang in my head
for days and days
and would not go away.

This is what I saw, looking over the Gallowgate,
Looking up from the city of death;
And I knew then that there would be a day of resurrection,
And I believe
that there will be a day of resurrection.[11]

Rituals

CHRIST IN THE CITY

Items needed

A large map of the area in which you live, some pens with luminous or fluorescent ink, a UV light.

Instructions for setting up

Cover the floor with the map. Put the pens beside the map. Set up the UV light near the map so that when it is switched on it will shine directly onto the map.

Description

Invite people to draw on the map one journey that they have made that week. The result will be a mass of sprawling tangled lines spreading across the city. This ritual could tie in with a service reflecting on the incarnation, on mission, on how Christ relates to the city. Christ lives in his people. So through them (though not exclusively through them) we can see that Christ is in the city. If you have used the luminous or fluorescent pens turn the main lights out and the UV light on. The lines will glow in the dark for a stunning effect.

Other ideas

Project images of your city around the worship space. The prayer "Jesus in the City" (pages 108–109) would also work well with this ritual.[12]

CUP OF SUFFERING

Items needed

Red wine vinegar, cup, cloth to wipe the cup.

Instructions for setting up

Set up a table with a glass of red wine vinegar and a cloth to wipe the cup.

Description

Invite people to drink from the cup if they are prepared to drink from the cup of suffering if that's what it takes to obey God and follow Christ.

This ritual clearly ties in with a service looking at Gethsemane.

Other ideas

You could also use the cup of suffering as part of a ritual standing in solidarity for those suffering round the world for their faith or any other situations of injustice.[13]

NAILS IN WOOD

Items needed

A large piece of wood—ideally driftwood or something similar—hammers, large nails.

Instructions for setting up

Place some nails and a few hammers on the ground next to the piece of wood.

Description

As an act of confession invite people to come and hammer a nail into the wood. During the confession play or sing a lament. The track "Protection" by Massive Attack (try the Brian Eno mix) which contains the line "Protection—you took the force of the blow" is a stunning track to play.

Other ideas

You could give people a nail to take away with them as a reminder.[14]

PLANT A SEED

Items needed

Seeds/bulbs, seed tray or small pots, soil/potting compost.

Instructions for setting up

If you are going to use the seed planting as a station that you invite people to come to, put soil, in a seed tray and seeds in a bowl next to it. If you are going to give everyone an individual pot and seed have a pile of pots, a bowl of soil, and a bowl of seeds.

Description

Invite people to plant a seed. This can be set up at a station where people come and plant the seed and leave it. Or it could be that they come and get a small pot and a seed/bulb and plant it to take home with them. When it flowers it will be a visual reminder of the ritual. At Easter a seed speaks of resurrection. The seed falls into the ground and has to die for new life to come from it.

Other ideas

Accompanying images of creation, plants, and new life would be good.
Another possible meaning is thinking about the creativity and gifts that God has given us that we can plant and use in the world.[15]

TENT STATION

Items needed

An inner tent (small tents usually have an inner tent that is see-through gauze and an outer waterproof sheet), pieces of cloth of varying degrees of thickness and opacity, a cross about a foot tall, Post-it notes, pens.

Instructions for setting up

Set up a small tent with just the inner tent on it so that you can see through the material. In the middle of the tent suspend a cross from the roof (it needs to be not too heavy!). On the outside of the inner tent place various pieces of material in patches. These pieces of material should be varying thicknesses and degrees of opacity. Try and project some light through the tent to highlight the cross. The idea is that you create the effect that as you move around the tent the cross is sometimes easily visible and sometimes obscured.

Description

Invite people to write their name on a Post-it note and stick it somewhere on the tent that represents where they see themselves in relation to God at the moment.

Other ideas

The tent is a very striking centerpiece that you could build a whole service around. It clearly lends itself to worship services at outdoor festivals or when camping.[16]

Renewing Culture

Talk of culture is a way of talking about how we live—what language we speak, what clothes we wear, what food we eat, what music we make or listen to, what kind of buildings we live in, what kind of rituals and religions we practice—culture has to do with how we live. And we are all born into a living stream of culture. Culture changes as we change—sometimes very slowly, sometimes very quickly. While human beings create culture, culture also creates us—we learn who we are and how to live, by growing up within a culture. Even the youngest child is being influenced by the culture all round it—where and how it was born—the language its parents are speaking to it, the way it is being dressed and so on.

Perhaps one of the most powerful ways in which our culture influences us is in the area of consumption. Our generation is becoming more and more aware of the damage we are doing to the planet. As Christians we believe that the basis of all culture is God's gift of creation—of the earth and everything in it. But the human race, and especially the rich industrialized nations in the North, are abusing that gift by consuming the earth's resources at an unsustainable rate. We are both producers of this culture and produced by it—with all our expectations about the kind of lifestyle we are entitled to.

Our culture is dominated by materialism. Our lives are often driven by the desire to earn more and have more—more stuff, more TV, more shopping. Not only does this happen at the expense of the planet, but huge numbers of people worldwide live in poverty, while a small minority consume a huge percentage of the world's wealth.

Meanwhile, our culture numbs us, makes us passive, and keeps us quiet. Every week, millions of us spend hours slumped in our chairs staring at the

TV screen. From the very earliest days of our lives we are constantly being encouraged to be good consumers—because our culture needs us to be. There's nothing wrong per se with shopping or consuming, but the balance, the ecology of consumption, is all wrong. Compared to the huge encouragement to be consumers of culture we are hardly encouraged to be creators of culture—we'd rather change channels than change the world.

Worship that is truly alt should renew our imagination by shaking us out of our numbness, by helping us to grieve for what is lost, and by helping us enter into a different story which imagines a new world, a new earth and heaven, with new possibilities for living. From our worship we should come away inspired to contribute to the creation of a redeemed culture, a culture of caring for the earth, a culture of justice, of good news for the poor.

The cross is the place where human culture is judged and condemned and forgiven by God, and the resurrection is God's great act of renewing culture—of changing how we live. When Paul reflected on knowing God through Jesus Christ, he said, "If anyone is in Christ, they are a new creation." The gift and call of God is that we are to know Christ and the power of resurrection—reactivating us and filling us with creative power. We are given a new way of looking at life, a way which is based in self-giving love and the justice of God. We are called into the new community of the church to be a sign together of new creation—we are called to challenge the powers which want to keep us quiet and complacent and to speak truth to them in the way Jesus did; we are called to find our worth and security in the love of God and in forgiving love for another, not in getting more and having more. Just as Jesus challenged the culture of his day, we who have the Spirit of Jesus in our lives are called to challenge and change our culture—our community and our worship are a sign of that—our words and music, our photography, our rituals, our democracy, our meetings—all of these are the beginnings of a creative challenge to ourselves and to our society. We will always be creations of our culture, but we are also called to be active and inspired and alive; our commitment to shaping and renewing culture is one of the signs that we believe in the resurrection.

Faithful Improvisation

Alt worship often tries to face in two or more directions at once. The project of introducing radical changes to how we worship has gone hand in hand with a positive re-evaluation of the role of tradition. In thinking about this negotiation between continuity and change, tradition and innovation, we have found Tom Wright's notion of faithful improvisation helpful.[17]

Imagine a missing Shakespeare play is found but with a scene missing. To put on the play the missing scene would have to be improvised by a theatre company. To improvise well, the actors would need to immerse themselves in the rest of the plot, the characters, and other Shakespeare works. The missing scene might be taken in a number of directions. But those who knew the play and the author would be able to judge whether the improvisation rang true to the story, whether it was faithful or not. Wright suggests that the Bible is like a drama in several acts—Act 1 Creation, Act 2 . . . and so on. Our task is to faithfully improvise the missing scene between Acts and the return of Christ. As with the example of actors improvising the scene in a play, not just any improvisation will do. Our improvisation will be judged by its faithfulness to the story and the author. But within this there is a whole range of imaginative possibilities.

This notion of faithful improvisation is very exciting for worship. It frees us from an authoritarian use of tradition, without losing the plot and saying that anything goes. Admittedly it's a harder one to call (who's to say if an improvisation is faithful or not?). It also places responsibility on the architects of new worship to be located in the Christian story. But the better an actor knows the plot and the better a musician knows the scales, the more freedom they will have to improvise. It's a skill that can be developed given the freedom to take some risks and make some mistakes along the way.

Part 4

Pentecost

Resources

Pentecost is now well off the map of most people's consciousness outside of the church. The ubiquitous contemporary fascination with "spirituality" is rarely focused by the Christian doctrine of the Holy Spirit. Yet this festival may be self-consciously growing in importance for many people within the church. Since the first waves of charismatic renewal in the 1960s and 1970s, a renewed awareness and experience of the work of the Holy Spirit has been seen as a key response to the crises and decline of the western church. The rise of Pentecostalism across the world has given this young tradition a strong profile within the world church.

Pentecost celebrates the story of the coming of the Holy Spirit to the first Christian disciples gathered in Jerusalem after the resurrection and ascension of Jesus Christ. The images of wind and fire from this story have marked the liturgies of Pentecost from the earliest days of Christian worship, alongside other biblical images of the Spirit: a dove, flowing water, and the breath of God.

The work of contemporary theologians such as Gustavo Gutiérrez and Jürgen Moltmann has forged new links between the language of "Spirit" and the language of "Life." Ecumenical theologians and liturgists highlight this founding story of the church through the work of the One Spirit as a stimulus for Christian unity. Theologians of liberation have brought new depths to the miracle of translation which unites people from differing cultural and linguistic backgrounds. Eco and feminist theology reflect on Paul's vision of the Spirit in Romans 8, sighing and groaning within creation as it longs for liberation and wholeness.

131

Marked by celebration and energy, this festival is also marked by urgency in its invocation of the Holy Spirit—Come Holy Spirit! The church cries to God for the life which is both within it and beyond it, in the name of Jesus who was raised by the power of this Spirit and who has promised to be ever present to the church through the coming of the Spirit.

Venite

Sing to God,
Our Strong Liberator,
Make a joyful noise,
And go to where God is;
Be thankful,
Sing and make joyful noise to celebrate God's worth.

God is great,
The Power above all powers,
The Maker of earth and sea and sky

Come to God in awe and wonder;
Kneel and worship God our Maker;
God is ours,
We are God's,
Alive in the world of God's love.[1]

Like the Wind

Lead: Like the wind which stirred the waters of creation
ALL: **God is moving in the world**

Lead: Like the holy fire burning in the desert
ALL: **God is living in the world**

Lead: Like the wind which drove back the waters of Exodus
ALL: **God is acting in the world**

Lead: Like the song welling up in the mouth of King David
ALL: **God is singing in the world**

Lead: Like the breath which stirred dry bones in the valley
ALL: **God is gathering in the world**

Lead: Like the angel filling Mary's body with light
ALL: **God is loving in the world**

Lead:	Like the cries of the Christ child to be fed in the night
ALL:	**God is coming into the world**

Lead:	Like the dove resting on the baptized Messiah
ALL:	**God is christening the world**

Lead:	Like the healing that comes from the hands of the Savior
ALL:	**God is mending life in the world**

Lead:	Like the voice of the Teacher in the ears of the crowd
ALL:	**God is speaking in the world**

Lead:	Like the last choking breath of a man on a cross
ALL:	**God is dying for the world**

Lead:	Like the silence that covers the tomb in the garden
ALL:	**God is waiting for the world**

Lead:	Like the power that raised Jesus Christ from the dead
ALL:	**God is rising in the world**

Lead:	Like the breath of the Christ on the skin of disciples
ALL:	**God is breathing on the world**

Lead:	Like the fire that falls on the Day of Pentecost
ALL:	**God is giving life to the world**[2]

Opening Doors

Eternal God,
fling open the doors of our hearts
to the weather of your Spirit.
Lead us out beneath the dancing sky and wind
across the stumbling ground of our reality
to where the sound of worship never ceases
and the view stretches further than the human eye can see.
Through Christ the faithful witness, Amen.[3]

Thirst

It's been a hot day.
You've been out in the heat,
Had nothing to drink
And are thirsty.

My soul thirsts for you, my body longs for you, in a dry and weary land
where there is no water.

What does it feel like to be thirsty?
Your mouth is dry,
You are weary,
Your whole body longs for water.

Come, all you who are thirsty, come to the waters . . .

Jesus feels like this traveling through Samaria on a hot day.
Tired from the journey he sits down by the well.
A Samaritan woman comes to draw water.
Jesus asks her for a drink.

Will you give me a drink?

Samaritans are distrusted by Jews.
Women are not to be approached in public:
She is surprised and asked why Jesus does this.
He replies

*If you knew the gift of God and who it is that asks you for a drink, you
would have asked him and he would have given you living water.*

Living water?
What's that?
How will Jesus get it without a bucket?

*Everyone who drinks this water (from the well) will be thirsty again, but who-
ever drinks the water I give will never thirst. Indeed, the water I give will
become in them a spring of water welling up to eternal life.*

Never be thirsty again . . .
A spring of water welling up to eternal life;
The woman asks for some of this water.
Think about your own thirst;
Imagine being with Jesus at the well as he speaks of this life-giving water;
It's freely available to all who are thirsty.

If anyone is thirsty let them come to me and drink . . .

Speak to Jesus
If you want to ask him for this water.

Cups of water will be brought round. Take some time to pray and ask God to
quench your thirst. Let this drink be the gift of God's life giving Spirit. As
you drink be refreshed.[4]

You Come to Us

We have been told that if we do this,
you will be here;
and we believe this.
Not because you are not here in every place and time,
Not because you are not with us always—
You will be here because this is your promise,
You will be here because this is your way.

*This is your way, to come to us
in the words of your story told again—
to come to us through memory.*

*This is your way, to come to us
in the signs of bread and wine,
to come to us through sight and touch and taste.*

This is your way, to come to us in Spirit,
Gently and powerfully gathering
memory and sight and touch and taste,
taking what we can do and see and know and making it more.

*This is your way—when bread is broken
and when wine is poured—
we are to know you have been dead for us.*

*This is your way—when bread is eaten
and when wine is drunk—
we are to know you are alive for us.*

*This is your way—when bread and wine are shared,
we are to know that you are one with us
and we are one with you.*

Jesus Christ, Word made Flesh,
as we do what you have called us to do,
come and keep your promise here.
As you gave thanks, so we give thanks.

God in holy community,
God who is three in one,
intimate and open God,
we thank you for opening your life to us.

Father and Mother of Creation
Lover of Life, Maker of all things,
We thank you for making us.

Jesus Christ, God come in the flesh,
Lover of body and soul,
Patient taker of time,
Impatient prophet of justice,
We thank you for giving your life for us.

Holy Spirit, God of Life,
Breath of life in all that lives,
Invisible comforter and restless provoker of our souls,
We thank you for bringing your life to us.

Jesus Christ, Alpha and Omega,
You are the one by whom all things were made,
The one in whom all things hold together.
You have been here for us
In Bethlehem and Nazareth,
In Galilee and Calvary,
We celebrate your life and death and life from death,
Believing you have risen to heaven's heights,
Yet still come near when bread is broken
and when wine is poured.

Now we pray, that in your own way
you will come to us,
Send your Holy Spirit,
Come to our minds in wisdom,
Come to our hearts in love,
Come to our souls in fire,
Come to our bodies in healing.

O Lord open our lips
And our lives shall receive your life.[5]

In This Place

In this place where heaven and earth meet
under the rainbow of God's promise
in this sharing of bread and wine
future hope becomes reality now

So bring your scorched earth
bring your harvest

bring your open sky
bring your restless guilty waters
bring your swift unbending road
bring your urgent inner city
to the table where your host says
"I make all things new"[6]

The Lord's Prayer

Our God in heaven,
Father and Mother to us,
We long for your holy name to be praised,
For life to be all you want and call it to be.
We ask you to give us the food we need today,
To forgive our debts,
As we forgive our debtors;
To lead us out of trouble,

And to free us from evil.
We pray to you, because you are the God
Whose right it is to have power,
Whose glory it is to use it for good,
Amen.[7]

We Believe in One God

We believe in one God
the Creator of all things,
who loves the whole creation
with a father's tenderness
and a mother's strength.

We believe in one God
our Liberator Jesus Christ
the Word of God made flesh
true God and truly human;
born among the poor he lived
as bringer of God's Kingdom;
a teacher and a healer
a lover of life and a prophet of justice,
forgiver of sins and a friend of sinners,
who welcomed the outcasts
and challenged the powerful,
Whose death on the cross
defeated sin and death,
Who rose from the dead

And is alive forever
in power and glory.

We believe in one God
the Holy Spirit, the giver of life
the Breath of life in all life
the gift of God to the people of God
Disturber and our Comforter.
The fire and the dove,
who makes us one community
in peace and love.

We believe in one God
a community of love
a trinity of holiness
the beginning and end
of all life, Amen.[8]

Doors

Lead: The kingdom of God has many points of entry, but they are
          not always in the places we expect.

          So we need to be alert and ready to enter any time, any place
          we may be called.

ALL: **We will enter the kingdom through the door marked
          "push."**

Lead: We will not give up if it doesn't open easily.

ALL: **We will enter the kingdom through the door marked
          "changing room."**

Lead: We will not attempt spiritual exercise in clothes that restrict
          our movements.

ALL: **We will enter the kingdom through the door marked "fire
          escape."**

Lead: We will not go back into smoke-filled rooms to rescue our
          possessions.

ALL: **We will enter the kingdom through the door marked "late
          night opening and all day Sundays."**

Lead: We will not restrict the times and places of access to God.

ALL: **We will enter the kingdom through the door marked "si-
           lence — recording in progress."**
Lead: We will not miss our part in God's symphony.

ALL: **We will enter the kingdom through the door marked "bar
           staff only."**
Lead: We will not ignore people who are thirsty.

ALL: **We will enter the kingdom through the door marked "hon-
           eymoon suite."**
Lead: We will not keep any part of ourselves from God's love.

ALL: **We will enter the kingdom through the door marked "to
           the cells."**
Lead: We will not plea-bargain to escape responsibility for our crimes.

ALL: **We will enter the kingdom through the door marked "lost
           property."**
Lead: We will not get rid of people who have not yet been claimed
           by their rightful owner.

ALL: **We will enter the kingdom through the door marked "guest
           list."**
Lead: We will not have forgotten to have our friends' names put on
           it too.

ALL: **We will enter the kingdom through the door marked
           "exit."**
Lead: We will not continue shopping while the manager puts the
           lights out.

ALL: **We will go through these doors in the power of the Spirit,
           knowing that Jesus has gone through them all first.**[9]

Rituals

Items needed

Anointing oil (this could be specially commissioned chrism or just massage or baby oil).

Instructions for setting up

If people are to be invited forward to receive anointing with oil then you need enough small bottles or bowls of oil for each of the places they will come to.

Description

Anointing with oil is a ritual that is usually associated with prayer for healing. It can also be used as an act of commissioning. Invite people to come and be anointed with oil. This could be done as people receive bread and wine in communion. Or it could be done separately. One way that works well is for the first person to be anointed and then take the oil and anoint the next person and so on. It helps convey communal responsibility and gifts rather than them being owned and controlled by the leaders or experts.

Anointing on the forehead is the traditional place, but if this feels too intimate for your group, then an alternative is to anoint the wrists.

Other ideas

Laying on of hands is also a ritual commonly associated with prayer for healing so you might like to offer people the opportunity for prayer in that way at the same time.[10]

WIND

Items needed

Several electric fans, some strips of muslin.

Instructions for setting up

Set up an area with several electric fans blowing. It will add to the effect to have some strips of light material hanging so that they are blown by the breeze—light muslin works well. You could also project slides onto the muslin.

Description

Invite people to go and stand in the space that you have created and to take some time to pray to receive afresh the gift of God's Spirit. At the entrance have a laminated copy of "the Beaufort scale."

Other ideas

A video loop of images of wind—washing blowing in the breeze, storms, and so on would work well with this station.[11]

BITTERSWEET RITUAL

Items needed

Something sweet to taste—a good example would be runny honey with bread sticks to dip in to taste, something bitter to taste—some chopped up pieces of lemon or some bitter herbs to dip in salt water (as is done in the Passover meal where the salt water represents the tears of the slaves).

Instructions for setting up

Set up an area with something sweet to taste and something bitter to taste.

Description

Invite the worshipers to reflect on their own journey of faith. Some will be full of thanks for good things that have happened, others will be struggling with hardships. If the former, they can taste the sweet as a way of giving thanks to God. If the latter, they can taste the bitter herbs to acknowledge the reality of their struggles before God. Some may want to do both. While this ritual takes place a good piece of music to accompany it is "Bittersweet Symphony" by the Verve (the James Lavelle remix on the single "The Drugs Don't Work" is the best version).

You can print some words of prayer in front of the sweet and bitter to help people as they reflect—

Sweet

Thanks for the gift of life
for the good things you give to us
we remember the joys and happiness
you never leave us
we shall journey in your presence as long as we live

Bitter

We acknowledge the reality of pain and suffering in life
often we cannot understand it and wonder where you are
we remember bitter and unhappy times
you never leave us
we shall journey in your presence as long as we live

Other ideas

This could be a good end-of-year ritual reflecting on the bitter and sweet in the year gone by. This could then be followed by sharing and praying about hopes and dreams for the new year and tying them on the Christmas tree.[12]

DRINKING WATER

Items needed

Cups or bottles of chilled water.

Instructions for setting up

Either set up some points around the room where people are invited to come to or have trays of water to distribute to where people are sitting.

Description

Invite people to drink to be filled afresh with God's Spirit, the living water described in John 4. If you can get the water chilled even better. This ritual follows the meditation "Thirst" (pages 133–134). In this case you could take drinks around to where people are sitting. Then give some time and space for prayer.

Other ideas

Images of water always work really well. Use slides or video loops to enhance the worship environment.[13]

FIRESTARTER

Items needed

Sparklers—enough for everyone to have one, matches or a taper, CD single of "Firestarter" by The Prodigy.

Instructions for setting up

Give everyone a sparkler.

Description

Light one sparkler. People can then light their sparklers from this one and pass it on. In no time at all everyone's sparklers will be lit. This ritual is a good end to a service where people are sent out to take the fire of God's Spirit as they go. It works well accompanied by the track "Firestarter" by The Prodigy (choose carefully which mix you choose—the Empirion mix on the single is the best).

Sparklers make quite a bit of smoke so you may need to go outside if there are smoke alarms or if you are in a building with a low ceiling.

Other ideas

Images of flames flickering look great. If you use the track "Firestarter" get someone to introduce the ritual and the idea of God being a Firestarter over the start of the track. This should be upbeat and loud.[14]

FROZEN

Items needed

A large block of ice (try finding a shop that sells ice for ice sculptures), some scaffolding, and chain to suspend the ice from, tea lights, small spot lights.

Instructions for setting up

This ritual requires a bit of extra effort to set up but is well worth it. Suspend the ice off the ground with some chains off a scaffolding pole. Project some lights on to it. You'll also need to put a plastic sheet underneath to protect the floor.

Description

Invite people to come and light a tea light and place it under the ice to contribute to its melting. This ritual could be part of some intercessions asking God to melt the cold hearts of leaders in situations of oppression or injustice. Or it could be a response asking God to melt the coldness of our own hearts.

Other ideas

A good addition is to record a dripping tap and play it quietly in the background. This also lends itself to some great images of water and ice. Get a video camera and video the ice melting and use that in future services.[15]

Incarnation and Popular Culture

Incarnation is about God becoming flesh in Jesus Christ. God's action offers a metaphor for worship that seeks to resonate in contemporary culture. Rather than shouting from a distance God chose to enter our experience and humanity, to become one of us so we could know and encounter God. This was done in a specific context—first-century Palestine with a particular language and cultural set of signs and symbols. Jesus communicated with the resources of the culture in which he was incarnate. We are called to do the same in our own cultural incarnation—"As the Father has sent me so I am sending you."

People use the cultural resources available to them to make meanings as they construct a sense of their own self and the social reality in which that self lives.

The metaphor of incarnation suggests that popular culture should resource the culture of our worship.

The arts have always had a crucial role to play in evoking the presence of the holy, functioning as "windows on eternity." This is particularly the case when in a well established religious tradition the conventional language of the sacred has become over-familiar—art opens up perception in new ways, enabling us to see the world with new eyes. Popular culture is heavily image-oriented and iconographic.

If the church's iconographic style ceases to be earthed in popular culture, while its imagery may still exert a powerful grip on hearts and minds, the dangers both of nostalgia and of otherworldliness become very real.

Some in the churches may dismiss the use of popular culture as bad taste or a gimmick. In part this is because a high/low view of culture still seems to be prevalent. But it's also because the cultural forms of church have become so normative that to insiders they are both the "natural" and the "correct" way of worshiping God. Culture has become an invisible part of the equation. In this reification, popular culture is simply "out of place" because it transgresses established symbolic boundaries. Television in church, for example, is not "natural."

The model of incarnation provokes the claim that a spiritual tradition needs to be continually renewing itself if it is to be faithful to its own tradition. Every revelation is initially culture bound: It speaks the language and uses the imagery of its own time and society. If it did not, communication would be impossible.

The transmission of the gospel and the mission of the church need to be reincarnated in every culture and historical moment. The Spirit of Pentecost is the Spirit of translation, enabling fresh and faithful incarnations of Christian practice in our times and places.

Reframing Tradition

In a post-modern culture tradition and continuity are essential gifts. Without tradition there would be no Christian faith. At a time when culture seems to be changing so fast, to be located in a 2000-year-old tradition gives a real sense of "weight," a much-needed anchor point in the world. Being located within the Christian tradition and seeking to be faithful to it helps to avoid group and individual beliefs becoming too subjective or personal — it offers a check on spirituality. It also turns out to be a tradition with a vast amount of resources and an incredible global network. The basic and seemingly obvious point about the Christian tradition is that it is living and not closed or completed. In this respect the use of "tradition" to defend the status quo is not faithful to Christian tradition at all. In this kind of scenario religious people are defending not tradition but traditionalism. One is living, the other is dead. Part of the process of carrying a tradition forward is struggling with it, engaging in its debates as to how its enquiries can be carried forward. A tradition needs diversity at its heart. In this respect while tradition does in some ways provide limits, it also gives the tools to liberate us from the way traditions have been used against us. Wherever the message of Jesus for today is distorted the tradition needs correction. To keep reforming religious tradition in a prophetic spirit is to be faithful. This reforming impulse is at the heart of the tradition. To deny it is "to disallow that subversive and dangerous memory of Jesus in the church."[16] Paradoxically it is resources from within the tradition itself which will subvert the inadequacies and injustices of religious traditions.[17] To preserve a tradition then is to understand what is at its heart and then re-present that in our own context. Alt worship groups are in this sense well located within the tradition, regarding the One they follow as the "Holy Subversive" and themselves when they are true to Him as "sanctified subversives."

100 Routes to Resourcing Your Worship
in the Spirit of Nick Hornby

10 CDs for Ambient/Instrumental Music

Brian Eno. *Apollo: Atmospheres and Soundtracks.* Editions E. G. Records, 1989.

Boards of Canada. *In a Beautiful Place out in the Country.* Warp Records, 2000.

Compilation. *A Journey into the Ambient Groove 2.* Island Records, 1995.

B. Howie. *Music for Babies.* Polydor, 1996.

Compilation. *Ambient Dub,* volume 4: *Jellyfish.* Beyond Records, 1995.

Compilation. *The Big Chill: Pipedreams.* Rumour Records, 1997.

Tosca. *Suzuki in Dub.* G-Stone Recordings, 2000.

Heights of Abraham. *Electric Hush.* Pork Recordings, 1995.

Two Lone Swordsmen. "Swimming Not Skimming." MCA/Warner Chappell, 1996.

Jan Garbarek and the Hilliard Ensemble. "Officium." ECM Records, 1994.

10 Books of Liturgy

Various. *Imaging the Word.* 3 vols. United Church Press, 1994, 1995 and 1996.

Wild Goose Worship Group. *A Wee Worship Book.* Wild Goose, 1999.

Jones, Linda, Annabel Shilson-Thomas and Bernadette Farrell. *Celebrating One World*. HarperCollins, 1998.

Northumbria Community. *Celtic Daily Prayer*. HarperCollins, 2000.

Janet Morley. *Bread of Tomorrow*. SPCK, 1992.

Janet Morley. *All Desires Known*. SPCK, 1992.

Cardenal, Ernesto. *Abide in Love*. Orbis, 1995.

Wallace, Sue. *Multisensory Prayer*. Scripture Union, 2000.

de Mello, Anthony. *Sadhana: A Way to God: Christian Exercises in Eastern Form*. Doubleday Image, 1984.

St. Hilda Community. *Women Included*. SPCK, 1991.

10 Tracks with Vocals

A Man Called Adam. "Easter Song." *Café del Mar*. volume 2. React, 1995.

Faithless. "God Is a DJ." *Sunday 8pm*. Cheeky Records, 1998.

Delerium. "Silence." Nettwerk Productions, 2000.

The Space Brothers. "Forgiven." Mercury, 1997.

Moodswings. "Redemption Song." *Café del Mar*. volume 3. React, 1996.

Attaboy. "New World." *Real Ibiza*. volume 2. React, 1999.

Mama Oliver. "Stoned Together (Passion Called Peace)." *Kruder Dorfmeister K + D Sessions*. G-Stone Records, 1998.

Lauryn Hill. "To Zion." *The Miseducation of Lauryn Hill*. Columbia, 1998.

U2. "Grace." *All That You Can't Leave Behind*. Polygram Records, 2000.

Gavin Bryars. *Jesus' Blood Never Failed Me Yet*. Point, 1993.

10 Books of Alt Worship Theory and Practice

Mike Riddell, Mark Pierson and Cathy Kirkpatrick. *The Prodigal Project*. SPCK, 2000.

Paul Roberts. *Alternative Worship and the Church of England*. Grove Books, 1999.

Kevin and Brian Draper. *Refreshing Worship*. BRF, 2000.

Mike Riddell. *Alt.spirit@metro.m3*. Lion, 1997.

Steve Collins, Jonny Baker and Kevin Draper. *Labyrinth Leader's Guide*. Proost, 2002.

Steve Collins and Jonny Baker. *Fresh Vital Worship*. Proost, 2000.

Pete Ward (ed.). *Mass Culture: The Eucharist and Mission in a Postmodern World*. BRF, 1999.

Sue Wallace. *Multisensory Church.* Scripture Union, 2002.
Sally Morgenthaler. *Worship Evangelism.* Zondervan, 1999.
Pete Ward, ed. *The Rite Stuff.* BRF, 2002.

10 Alt Worship CDs

Proost. *Alternative Worship.* Proost, 2002.
LLS. *Music from the Late Late Service.* volumes 1–5. Sticky Music.
Grace. *Grace.* Proost, 1997.
Various. *Eucharist.* Proost, 1999.
Various. *Labyrinth Music and Meditations.* Proost, 2000.
Visions. *Unspoken Prayers.* Visions, 2000.
Visions. *Chants for Visions.* (taken from various Visions albums—available at www.mp3.com/abbess.
Synergy. *Return to Ritual.* Word, 1995.
Revive. *Beautiful Day.* Word, 1998.
Host. *Collect.* Host, 2001 (see www.altworship.org.uk)

10 Art Books

Jane Dillenberger. *Religious Art of Andy Warhol.* Continuum, 1998.
David A. Ross. *Bill Viola.* Whitney Museum of Art, 1998.
Hermann Kern. *Through the Labyrinth.* Prestel, 2000.
Alexandra Munroe with Jon Hendricks. *Yes Yoko Ono.* Harry N. Abrams, 2000.
Crucifixion, Descent, Ascension, Last Supper. Phaidon, 2000.
Sean Perkins, ed. *Experience.* Booth Clibborn Editions, 1995.
Lewis Hyde. *Trickster Makes This World.* North Point Press, 1998.
Yann Bertrand. *The Earth From the Air: 365 Days.* Thames & Hudson, 2001.
H. R. Weber. *On s Friday Noon.* SPCK, 1979.
Ann Goldstein. *Barbara Kruger.* Museum of Contemporary Art, 1999.

10 Image Sources

One Small Barking Dog, *Images for Worship Videos/DVD/CD-Rom*, volumes 1, 2, 3 (OSBD—see www.osbd.org)
One Small Barking Dog, *Journey* (OSBD, 2002)
Flicker, *Alternative Worship* (Flicker, 2002—see www.flickerweb.co.uk)

Visions, *Visions: Loops 1* (Visions, 2001—see www.visions-york.org)

Various, *Scriptorium web site* (free downloads at www.the-scriptorium.org)

St. Paul's Multimedia, *The Prodigal Son* slide set (St Paul's Multimedia)

CMS and USPG, *The Christ We Share*, pack of 32 images of Christ from cultures around the world (CMS and USPG—see www.cms-uk.org)

Steve Collins, Small Fire web site, collection of pictures of alternativeworship services www.smallfire.org)

1Giantleap, *1Giantleap* DVD (Palm Pictures, 2002)

Hexstatic, *Rewind*, CD-Rom that accompanies CD (Ninja, 2000)

10 Books on Contemporary Culture

Naomi Klein. *No Logo.* Flamingo, 2000.

Tom Sine. *Mustard Seed vs McWorld.* Baker Books, 1999.

Kalle Lasn. *Culture Jamming.* Quill, 2000.

Bill Brewster and Frank Broughton. *Last Night a DJ Saved My Life.* Headline, 1999.

John Storey. *Cultural Consumption and Everyday Life.* Arnold, 1999.

Zygmunt Bauman. *Postmodernity and Its Discontents.* Polity Press, 1997.

Rem Koolhaas and Bruce Mau. *S M L XL.* Penguin USA, 1998.

Jane Pavitt, ed. *Brand New.* V & A Publications, 2000.

Anita Roddick. *Take It Personally.* Thorsons, 2001.

Douglas Coupland. *Girlfriend in a Coma.* HarperCollins, 2000.

10 Websites

www.alternativeworship.org

www.proost.co.uk

www.the-scriptorium.org

www.freshworship.org

www.labyrinth.org.uk

www.osbd.org

www.flickerweb.co.uk

http://seaspray.trinity-bris.ac.uk/~altwfaq/

www.smallfire.org

http://jonnybaker.blogspot.com

10 Books of Contemporary Theology and Mission

Jürgen Moltmann. *The Source of Life*. Fortress, 1997.

Walter Brueggemann. *The Bible and Postmodern Imagination: Texts Under Negotiation*. Fortress, 1993.

Gustavo Gutiérrez. *The God of Life*. Orbis, 1991.

John Drane. *The McDonaldization of the Church*. Smith & Helwys, 2002.

Mike Riddell. *Threshold of the Future*. SPCK, 1998.

Tom Beaudoin. *Virtual Faith*. Jossey Bass, 1998.

Matthew Fox. *Original Blessing*. Bear and Co., 1983.

Robert Beckford. *Jesus Is Dread*. Darton, Longman & Todd, 1998.

Rodney Clapp. *Border Crossings*. Brazos Press, 2000.

Alan Jamieson. *Churchless Faith*. SPCK, 2002.

Notes

Foreword

1. The North American Society of Church Growth, 1996.
2. Richard Morin, *Washington Post*, May 1998.
3. C. Kirk Hadaway and P. L. Marler, "Did You Really Go to Church This Week? Behind the Poll Data," *The Christian Century*, May 6, 1998: 472–75.
4. George H. Gallup Jr., "Public Give Religion Its Lowest Ratings," Gallup Poll Tuesday Morning Briefing, Religion and Values, http://www.gallup.com January 7, 2003.
5. George Barna, "Surprisingly Few Adults Outside of Christianity Have Positive Views of Christians," Barna Research Online, http://www.barna.org/cgi-bin/PagePres sRelease.asp?PressReleaseID=127&Reference=D December 3, 2002.

Introduction

1. On this see Andrew Wilson-Dickson, *The Story of Christian Music* (Oxford: Lion, 1992), Chapter 46, "The Popular Stream." Wilson-Dickson suggests that Sunday school chorus books published in the 1920s and 1930s are reminiscent of the heyday of the music hall twenty years earlier, while youth song books of the 1960s betray the interests of their adult compilers and bear little relation to the secular youth music of the time (Beatles, Rolling Stones).
2. A North American edition of this influential book was recently published. See Dave Tomlinson, *The Post-Evangelical* (Grand Rapids: Zondervan, 2003).
3. See www.adbusters.org
4. Richard Bauckham, *The Theology of the Book of Revelation* (Cambridge: Cambridge University Press, 1993).

154

5. Paul Roberts, *Alternative Worship in the Church of England* (Grove Booklet W 155, 1999).

6. The last chapter of John Drane, *What Is the New Age Saying to the Church?* (London: Marshall Pickering, 1991) reads like a program for setting up alternative-worship groups.

7. Kenneth Lawrence, Jane Cather Weaver, and Roger Weddell (eds), *Imaging the Word*, vols 1–3 (Cleveland: United Church Press, 1994–1996).

Part 1: Advent and Christmas

1. "Call to Worship," Jonny Baker.
2. "Bethlehem," Doug Gay.
3. "God Waits," Steve Collins.
4. "Waiting," Vaux, London.
5. "Light Meditation," Steve Collins.
6. "The Starlit Darkness," Jonny Baker.
7. "Logos," Doug Gay.
8. "Matthew Says—Abraham Begat," Doug Gay.
9. "Matthew Says—Hail Joseph," Doug Gay.
10. "The Great Reversal," Vaux, London.
11. "Come and Be Born in Us," Doug Gay, Late, Late Service.
12. "Christmas Communion Thanksgiving," Doug Gay.
13. "The Sign Communion—We Bring Gifts," Doug Gay.
14. "We Believe in One God," Doug Gay.
15. "I Believe in God," Matt Patterson.
16. "Adventure of Reality," Steve Collins.
17. "The Sign," HOST/Russ Taylor/Doug Gay.
18. "Sleeping Bag," Steve Collins.
19. "Candle Lighting," Jonny Baker/Grace.
20. "Darkness and Light," Jonny Baker/Grace.
21. "Incense," Jonny Baker/Grace.
22. "Wailing Wall," Jonny Baker.
23. "Walking a Labyrinth," Jonny Baker.
24. "Christ Present in Culture," Jonny Baker/Grace.
25. "Icons of the Present," Jonny Baker/Grace.
26. "The Rabbit Hole," Jonny Baker.
27. "Great Reversal," Vaux, London.
28. From the Grace booklet "Fresh Vital Worship" by Steve Collins and Jonny Baker.
29. "Embodiment and Incarnation" was the title of the 1996 Aquinas lecture given by Murray, which contained these themes. It is cited in Melvyn Matthews, *Both Alike to Thee* (London: SPCK, 2000), pp. 53–55.
30. Eugene H. Peterson, *The Message* (Colorado Springs, CO: NavPress, 1993).

Part 2: Lent

1. "Into the Desert," Doug Gay. Matthew 4:1 and Matthew 6:6 are from, or adapted from, The New King James Version of the Bible. Hosea 2:14 is Doug Gay's paraphrase.
2. "An Approach to God—Losing My Religion," Doug Gay.
3. "Prodigal Returns," Tracy Wheeler.
4. "Prodigal's Brother," Adrian Riley.
5. "Prodigal Confession," Steve Collins.
6. "Impression," Martin Wroe.
7. "Arable Parable," Sanctuary, Bath.
8. "Do You Want to Be Healed?," Doug Gay/HOST.
9. "Jesus Give Us Courage," Doug Gay/Rachel Morley/HOST.
10. "Lent Identity," Steve Collins.
11. "Noise," Steve Collins.
12. "Reading the Bible," Steve Collins.
13. "Promised Land," Steve Collins.
14. "Big Confession," Rachel Morley/HOST.
15. "We Are Hungry," Doug Gay.
16. "You Are Hungry," Doug Gay.
17. "I Believe in Jesus," Doug Gay.
18. "Closing Blessing—Losing My Religion," Doug Gay.
19. "End Prayer," Steve Collins
20. "Distractions," Steve Collins.
21. "Contemporary Desert," Jonny Baker/Grace.
22. "Finding Identity in the Desert," Jonny Baker/Grace.
23. "Impression," Jonny Baker/Grace.
24. "Imposition of Ashes," Jonny Baker/Grace.
25. "Prayers in Sand," Jonny Baker/Grace.
26. "Sand and Water," Jonny Baker/Grace.
27. "Letting Go," Jonny Baker, Kev, Ana, and Brian Draper.
28. "Breathing." There are lots of variations on this. See Anthony de Mello's book *Sadhana: A Way to God* (New York: Doubleday, 1978) for some other ways of praying.
29. "Hands," Jonny Baker.
30. See Ian Fraser's book *Reinventing Theology as the People's Work* (Glasgow: Wild Goose, 1988).
31. From the Grace booklet "Fresh Vital Worship" by Steve Collins and Jonny Baker.

Part 3: Easter

1. "Psalm 118," translated by Steve Collins.
2. "God on a Stick," Paul Hobbs.
3. "The Guest," Brian Draper.
4. "Host," Brian Draper.

5. "Let There Be Exodus," Doug Gay.

6. "Jesus in the City," Doug Gay.

7. "Gethsemane," Tracy Wheeler and Tim Nickels. The Scripture quotations are from the NIV.

8. "John 21 Meditation," Steve Collins.

9. "Eucharist—Hospitality," Jonny Baker, incorporating confession by Kev, Ana, and Brian Draper and invitation by Mike Riddell. The Scripture quotations are from Eugene Peterson's paraphrase *The Message* (Colorado Springs, CO: NavPress, 1993).

10. "We Believe in Life," Doug Gay.

11. "The New Glasgow," Doug Gay.

12. "Christ in the City," Vaux—originally part of their "urban mass."

13. "Cup of Suffering," Jonny Baker/Grace.

14. "Nails in Wood," Jonny Baker/Grace.

15. "Plant a Seed," Jonny Baker/Grace.

16. "Tent Station," Resonance—a worship group based in Bristol.

17. For a fuller treatment of this, see N. T. Wright, *The New Testament and the People of God* (London: SPCK, 1992), pp. 140–43.

Part 4: Pentecost

1. "Venite," Doug Gay.

2. "Like the Wind," Doug Gay.

3. "Opening Doors," Steve Collins.

4. "Thirst," Jonny Baker. The Scripture quotations are from Psalm 63:1, Isaiah 55:1, John 4:7, John 4:10, John 4:13–14 (adapted), John 7:37 (adapted) (NIV).

5. "You Come to Us," Doug Gay.

6. "In This Place," Steve Collins.

7. "The Lord's Prayer," Doug Gay.

8. "We Believe in One God," Doug Gay.

9. "Doors," Steve Collins (after A. Thornton).

10. "Anointing with Oil," Jonny Baker/Grace.

11. "Wind," Jonny Baker/Grace.

12. "Bittersweet Ritual," Jonny Baker/Grace.

13. "Drinking Water," Jonny Baker/Grace.

14. "Firestarter," Jonny Baker/Grace.

15. "Frozen," Jonny Baker/Grace.

16. David Tracy, *The Analogical Imagination: Christian Theology and the Culture of Pluralism* (Crossroad Publishing, 1991), p. 324.

17. Tom Beaudoin, *Virtual Faith* (Jossey Bass, 1998), p. 154.

Index

158

Jonny Baker has been involved in youth ministry for fifteen years and is currently the National Youth Coordinator in the UK for the Church Mission Society. He is a member of Grace, an alt worship community in west London, and part of the wider alt worship scene in the UK. Jonny has coordinated the worship at Greenbelt Arts Festival for several years and is involved in various creative projects, including Labyrinth, which he helped to design and which was installed at St. Paul's Cathedral, London, in 2000. A songwriter and director of an independent record label, he has contributed to several alt worship albums. Jonny recently completed an MA in Youth Ministry and Applied Theology at King's College, London.

Doug Gay is studying for a PhD in Practical Theology at the University of Edinburgh in Scotland. An ordained minister in the United Reformed Church, he was a youth worker and housing worker before training for the ministry. He has lived, worked, and worshiped in east London and Glasgow. Doug was a founder of the Late, Late Service in Glasgow and the HOST congregation in London and was also a board member of Greenbelt Arts Festival. Committed to urban mission, he is passionate about theology and is an enthusiast for Christian involvement in the arts. Doug is a musician, songwriter, and hymn writer and was a regular religious columnist for *The Times*. He currently lives in rural Galloway in Scotland with his wife and three children.

Jenny Brown is an interactive media designer who has worked on a variety of CD-ROM and web-based projects. A founder-creator of the emberdays project on www.embody.co.uk, she has been involved in several alt worship communities since 1994.